The Tech Professional's Guide to Communicating in a Global Workplace

Adapting Across Cultural and Gender Boundaries

April Wells

WITHDRAWN

Apress®

The Tech Professional's Guide to Communicating in a Global Workplace

April Wells
Strongsville, Ohio, USA

ISBN-13 (pbk): 978-1-4842-3470-9   ISBN-13 (electronic): 978-1-4842-3471-6
https://doi.org/10.1007/978-1-4842-3471-6

Library of Congress Control Number: 2018934697

Managing Director, Apress Media LLC: Welmoed Spahr
Acquisitions Editor: Jonathan Gennick
Development Editor: Laura Berendson
Coordinating Editor: Jill Balzano

Cover designed by eStudioCalamar

Cover image designed by Freepik (www.freepik.com)

Distributed to the book trade worldwide by Springer Science+Business Media New York, 233 Spring Street, 6th Floor, New York, NY 10013. Phone 1-800-SPRINGER, fax (201) 348-4505, e-mail orders-ny@springer-sbm.com, or visit www.springeronline.com. Apress Media, LLC is a California LLC and the sole member (owner) is Springer Science + Business Media Finance Inc (SSBM Finance Inc). SSBM Finance Inc is a **Delaware** corporation.

For information on translations, please e-mail rights@apress.com, or visit www.apress.com/rights-permissions.

Apress titles may be purchased in bulk for academic, corporate, or promotional use. eBook versions and licenses are also available for most titles. For more information, reference our Print and eBook Bulk Sales web page at www.apress.com/bulk-sales.

Any source code or other supplementary material referenced by the author in this book is available to readers on GitHub via the book's product page, located at www.apress.com/9781484234709. For more detailed information, please visit www.apress.com/source-code.

Printed on acid-free paper

This book is dedicated to my husband, Larry Wells. Without his support and gentle prodding over the years, this book would never have been possible. He's kept me going and kept me focused even when I wanted to give up. It is because of him that I have had the opportunity to learn about so many different cultures from all over the world, including right next door.

About IOUG Press

*IOUG Press is a joint effort by the **Independent Oracle Users Group (the IOUG)** and **Apress** to deliver some of the highest-quality content possible on Oracle Database and related topics. The IOUG is the world's leading, independent organization for professional users of Oracle products. Apress is a leading, independent technical publisher known for developing high-quality, no-fluff content for serious technology professionals. The IOUG and Apress have joined forces in IOUG Press to provide the best content and publishing opportunities to working professionals who use Oracle products.*

Our shared goals include:

- Developing content with excellence
- Helping working professionals to succeed
- Providing authoring and reviewing opportunities
- Networking and raising the profiles of authors and readers

To learn more about Apress, visit our website at **www.apress.com**. Follow the link for IOUG Press to see the great content that is now available on a wide range of topics that matter to those in Oracle's technology sphere.

Visit **www.ioug.org** to learn more about the Independent Oracle Users Group and its mission. Consider joining if you haven't already. Review the many benefits at www.ioug.org/join. Become a member. Get involved with peers. Boost your career.

www.ioug.org/join

Table of Contents

About the Author

April Wells has been in IT for more than 20 years. She is an Oracle database administrator and applications DBA with experience in large companies, midsize companies, and startups. She has international experience in many regions of the world, including South America, Europe, Asia, Africa, and North America. April's international work has brought her into contact with people from all levels of organization and all walks of life, impressing upon her the need to adapt to better facilitate effective communication across cultures, ages, and genders. She has made many mistakes and learned much the hard way so that you don't have to.

Acknowledgments

Many thanks to the people who helped make this book possible. No one is an island, and no one does anything without the support and input of many others.

To family who have put up with my stupid hours and my inability to spend time with them even when they needed me the most...thank you. To my husband Larry... Thank you for pushing me when I needed pushed and being my cheerleader when I was feeling down. I finished because of you.. There were times you were certain that you would never live to see this published. I'm forever grateful to have you here beside me.

To the people I've worked with in the variety of countries and cultures I've been sent to work...thank you.

To the people who have gently, and not so gently, pointed out my mistakes and miss steps, thank you.

To the ASL teacher in Round Rock, Texas, who taught me how to listen with my eyes and my heart when ears don't always hear so well...thank you.

To Jonathan, Laura, and Jill at Apress who have held my hand and kicked my behind and walked with me the entire way...thank you.

CHAPTER 1

Communication Matters

Everyone communicates. By learning to communicate more effectively and efficiently, you can become a more valuable employee, improve your self-confidence, and increase your worth to your department and your company. As technologists, we are often better at communicating with the people who we see every day, but I know from experience (you know, those hits you take on your performance appraisals that suggest you could improve in your communication skills?) that we can improve in the way we interact with just about everyone we meet.

We all communicate, and we all have from the day we took our first breath. We continue to communicate until we take our final breath. Any parent understands the difference between the "I'm wet" cry, the "I'm hungry" cry, and the "I'm bored" cry. You can glean from across distances at least some of the information that someone is trying to convey to you even without being able to hear them.

You know when your boss is late for a meeting, and you know when your loved ones are in a bad mood.

Communication happens on an almost continual basis. By learning to communicate in different situations in the most effective way, you can further your career and make your next performance appraisal better. Pay attention to the different communication situations you find yourself in and learn how to adapt your message and method to the current situation.

1

© April Wells 2018
A. Wells, *The Tech Professional's Guide to Communicating in a Global Workplace*,
https://doi.org/10.1007/978-1-4842-3471-6_1

I've been reminded of the criticality of communicating effectively in a business setting when I've gotten my annual performance appraisal and heard that communication was one of the places I needed to concentrate my efforts for the following year. I've read the appraisals and worked at improving in one or another place where I thought my communication has been lacking. It was hard to listen to that boss, however, tell me how much I was lacking in communication ability when he was the one who repeatedly called me into his office to look over his critical e-mails to make sure there weren't any glaring factual, grammar, or other mistakes. If I was so abysmal at communication, I'm not sure I was the best person to do the proofreading and make suggestions. I was never quite sure what I was supposed to do with the mixed messages I was getting, but I helped with the emails to make my boss look good, and I worked hard to improve the preception that everyone had of my communication skills.

I read books.

I watched videos and Ted talks.

I researched where I thought I might be lacking and I learned. And as I learned my performance appraisals improved and soon I no longer was getting told that it was a weakness I needed to improve upon. It became one of my strengths and selling points.

This book contains a great deal of what I learned through all of those methods and through much trial and error. May you learn from my mistakes.

Terminology

When you are talking about any topic that you aren't well versed in, you need to understand the vocabulary that is common to that topic. Ironically, the best place to start this conversation on communication is with the basic vocabulary that we will use in this book. This will set us off on a good common ground of using the same words and them meaning the same thing.

Communication

Communication isn't something that magically happened when we started our professional career. It has been going on all of our lives. We do it every minute of every day, and usually we do it without thinking about doing it. We simply communicate.

When people think about *communication*, they typically think about the spoken word, be it face to face or across a telephone line. Communication isn't merely speaking with others, though. It is more than that.

A little better, but not complete. Lets look a little closer at communication in more of its forms.

Communication can take many forms, one of which is of course the spoken word. But think about all of the ways that you exchange information every day.

You wake up in the morning, you talk to your family over breakfast, you look at your text messages, you check e-mail, and you may look at social media. All of these things are communication.

If you drive to work, you play the nonverbal communication game of navigating traffic. You merge onto the highway, you nod or motion to people crossing the street, and you yield the right of way or you don't. Stopping for coffee or breakfast on your way to work? You communicate with the clerk who waits on you or with the counter attendant at the gas station. If you take a cab or public transportation to work, you flag down the transportation, you speak to the driver, and maybe you tell him where you need to go or you simply nod and smile to her when you climb the steps. You pull the cord when you need the bus to stop. You mumble "good morning" to your fellow passengers.

At work, you check your voice mail, check your e-mail, IM your teammates, and start your day. You sit in meetings and listen or participate; you take notes.

Going out at lunch for a walk? Did you notice the lone protestor in the park? What about the woman singing outside in the park with her guitar case open? Maybe the panhandler on the corner? They're all communicating too.

You communicate all of your waking hours all of your life in one way or another, sometimes one on one, sometimes in a small group, and sometimes with everyone you can possibly reach with your message.

Books, newspapers, magazines, those annoying flyers that someone puts under the windshield wipers of cars when people are shopping...all of these things are communication.

Think about the communication you experienced today and pay attention to what you experience tomorrow. Think about what is effective and what isn't, what gets the point across, and what just leaves you feeling a bit wrong.

Culture

So, if that is communication, what is culture?

Culture is the particular set of customs, morals, codes, and traditions of a person or group.

Frequently people think about culture as being "mine" or "theirs." Often this is with the connotation that because "mine" is what the person is comfortable with, it has to inherently be better than "theirs." But...if you are on the other side of the equation (the "theirs" side), you simply have a different "mine" perspective. Usually the "theirs" side is the people who live in another country. This, however, isn't always the case.

Think about the people you come into contact with every day. Are they just like you? None of them is just like me. Even identical twins have their own culture because they have their own set of experiences that make parts of them unique between themselves.

If I take stock of myself for just two minutes, here's what I come up with:

I am...

A woman

A writer

Middle aged

Middle class

Sister, daughter, wife, mother of two

Caucasian

The youngest

And the oldest (I was adopted by my grandparents... another unique culture... so I was my biological mother's oldest and my adopted mother's <biological grandmother's> youngest)

I was born...

in Western Pennsylvania

into a blue-collar family

I grew up...

In a small town

On a farm

As the youngest child

As a tomboy

I live...

In a suburb

In a single-family home that I own

With my husband and our grown children

With a dog and a cat

25 miles from where I work

In a middle-class neighborhood

In school I was...

In the top 10 percent of my graduating class

A nontraditional college student

Awarded a BS in information science (with a math and computer science minor and almost an English minor) in two years and three months

For my career...

I work in IT

I can program Cobol

I'm an apps DBA

These are pieces of my culture. I can no more change most of them than I can change who I fundamentally am. And even the ones that I can change, I still will be fundamentally me as long as I live.

Where you were born and grew up are part of your culture. Your point of view on many things has been formed because you grew up in a big city or in a small town, in an affluent neighborhood or in abject poverty, as an only child or with siblings. The things you have been exposed to are part of your culture. The things that you have chosen to expose yourself to are as well.

But what about the department you work in? What about the career path you are on and where on that path you find yourself? Those are part of your culture too, particularly when it comes to many facets of communication.

Building Trust

Communication is essential to building trust, and trust is essential in creating relationships, business relationships, casual relationships, and any relationships.

Think of a time when you have been working on a project and you have needed to rely on other people to help you get it done. Rarely are there projects in a business environment where we can do the entire project alone. We nearly always need to rely on someone else, often a large team, to accomplish the business goal. You likely learned early in the project that there were people who communicated better than others and some who rarely communicated at all.

People who communicate rarely if ever unless prodded into it are usually the ones who you end up feeling can't be trusted. You never know what their status is in a project, and you don't know if their deliverables are running on schedule or if they are behind due to difficulties or need help from someone else on the team or from external expertise to complete milestone tasks.

We all know people who are perpetually late for meetings, even the meetings that they scheduled.

Without open communication, it's easy to fall behind in project deliverables or to have to hurry and work long into the night because someone has forgotten to tell you what their requirements are. You might even end up looking bad because your requirements are dependent on someone else to deliver something to you and you must make that deliverable an emergency because timelines were not communicated to you in a timely manner. The trust someone has in you has faltered because you in turn were not able to trust the person on whom you relied for information.

Cultural Differences

It's important not to get caught up in thinking that cultural differences matter only if you are communicating with someone from a different country. While, particularly in IT, there are many different global cultures that work elbow to elbow, these are not the only ones you work with, meet with, and come into contact with every day. Learning how to communicate with different cultures makes a world of difference.

For example, there are vast cultural differences between people who were born in the 1950's and 60's and lived through the early years of computers with thier punch cards, Apple IIe and storing your program on a casette tape (Baby Boomers into Generation X-ers) and people who are just now entering the workplace (Millennials). Those of us who have worked through different technologies and different programming methods and languages often speak different languages. For instance, Agile projects are very different from Waterfall projects. Java is, often, as foreign a language to someone who learned programming with Cobol or C++ as Portuguese is for someone who speaks only English. Bridging these cultural differences may not make any difference monetarily, but it can be a huge difference in making your workday easier and your work environment less stressful.

People at different ends of their career path (those coming into the department versus those nearing retirement) have a different culture too.

They have a different background, a different way to view their career, and a different set of priorities. Again, communicating across these cultural differences can make your daily life less stressful.

Look for these differences. You will find yourself with the reputation for being able to communicate effectively, and people will seek you out as someone with whom they are comfortable working.

Why Communication Matters

So, why does it matter, and why should it matter to you specifically? It matters because by stopping and thinking you can change the way you interact with your peers, the people who you report to, and the people who look to you for guidance. By thinking about cultural differences, you can change other people's perceptions of you and can further your career on whatever path it is taking you.

I've been fortunate. I've gotten to travel, with my family or for work, rather extensively. Through my travels, I've gotten to stop and look at the differences in people, and I've learned some valuable lessons about communication.

Learning Even a Few Words in a New Language Can Make a Difference

People like to hear their native language, even if you don't get it quite right. Non-native speakers sometimes believe that if they are not fluent in a language, there is no sense in trying to use anything they might know. If you know you are going to be traveling to a country where you are a non-native or nonfluent speaker, learn a few key words. *Hello, good-bye, please, thank you, where is the bathroom?* are good ones to know. People will make the extra effort to help you if they see that you are trying.

When we went to France, we went to a global amusement park. We were advised that people love to hear their native language and that they are impressed if you can attempt to converse with them.

When I went to talk to someone at one of the rides to ask a question, the woman was so impressed that I was polite and I was able to say hello to her and to struggle with some other words to ask the question. The smile on her face was astounding. She admitted she could speak fluent English but was impressed at my attempts. She gave me a rare pin from her own lanyard, free meal tickets for lunch, and a stuffed animal for my daughter, all because I had been polite and tried to speak to her in her native language.

Ask Questions to People Who You Trust Who Understand the Culture

Sometimes it can be costly to not understand local language and even more so to not understand the local culture. There is the culture that applies to people who live in the country, and there is the culture that applies only to people visiting the country, and if you don't have a basic understanding of what is expected of visitors, it can really affect your bottom line.

Think that communication and cultures aren't important to your pocketbook? When we were visiting Vietnam, we again went exploring. My son, by this time, was an adult but looked older than he was. He decided to go out exploring in the morning before the group (again, a tour group) left the hotel. A cab driver flagged him over and motioned him (with a huge grin) into his cab (which was simply a black buggy on the back of the bike). Fees were not discussed, and there was nothing on his vehicle that would have led Adam to believe that he was anything other than someone working for the hotel for the guests to use. He had enough currency to tip the man well, and he was confident that the ride would be worth it. The driver then proceeded to take Adam on a tour of some of the interesting temples in the neighborhood. When Adam was delivered back to the front door of the hotel, the driver demanded what amounted to about $100 US and was trying to get Adam to understand that he needed to pay. The local guide assigned to our trip argued with the driver, and the fee was drastically reduced (by a bit more than half). The driver made $45 US for a 30-minute trip, and Adam learned a valuable lesson in communication and the difference in understanding when communication doesn't happen.

It's Not Good, It's Not Bad, It's Just Different

People have a tendency to be a little judgmental of things that they don't understand or to which they haven't been exposed. Being obviously judgmental can affect your reputation if not your pocketbook, and sometimes a good reputation and goodwill value are more important than money.

People can see when you are reluctant to engage in customs that you aren't comfortable with and can hold that against you. Worse, if you are representing your company, they can hold it against the company you represent. The bad feelings that they hold because of what they see to be judgment of their culture could mean the difference between them doing business with your company or not doing business with it. More important, though, they are likely to share their opinions with other people they know (including business acquaintances), which can impact your reputation.

South Africa taught me how hung up people in the United States can be on words and labels. One of our tour guides while there was Supa, a man who was honest and forthright. He taught me that no matter how dismal the townships might look to an outsider, they are much better than the places where the immigrants (who mostly make up the population of the townships) came from.

From him I also learned that words can hold power, but they don't have to. Words like *black person, white person,* or *colored person* might hold implications to someone in another culture or another country. In South Africa, a black person is the progeny of black parents, a white person is the progeny of white parents, and a colored person is simply someone of mixed heritage. Their parents and ancestors might be black, white, Asian, Indian, Japanese, or any other mixture of ethnic backgrounds. Again, it is easy to slight someone else's culture by taking offense to words or attitudes that are different from your own.

Don't Take Yourself Too Seriously

There are times when you deal with people of different cultures when everything has to be all business, and those times, by definition, need to happen. You go to a country on business, you go into the offices and discuss what needs to be discussed, and you make the business deals you need to make. You remember to use the words that make the best impression and respect the customs of the culture.

But what happens at the end of the day, when the business day is done and you are invited to enjoy the local recreation? I've heard, often, that the best business deals are made on the golf course rather than in the boardroom. People like to spend time outside of the formal setting. If you can jump into the culture with both feet and not worry about being formal all of the time, you can make lasting connections with the people you are working with.

Business people remember this. It's part of the way they work every day. Oftentimes people in IT tend to immerse themselves in technology and aren't always willing to spend time playing. But people who have different cultures (globally or otherwise) know things that you don't, and being able to reach out to these people later can help you answer questions on things you don't even know you don't know yet.

12

From England I learned that it is always a good thing to be true to yourself. The tour group we traveled with over several years brought the brighter, better, safer side to the people in the group. As a family, we are unique and a little on the adventuresome side. We found some of the most interesting places when we were on our own, and we never hesitated to share where we went or what we found there. This meant that when we asked the local guide where we could go on a free afternoon that wasn't too far or too time-consuming to get to, he suggested that our family might enjoy Camden Town. It was awesome. It was a little unusual, and we completely understood the guide's comment that he would not have suggested it to most of the people on the tour. If we would not have been willing to let our weird side show, we would have missed out on seeing some of the more interesting aspects of London's suburbs.

In addition, understanding how our words are heard is often key to our being able to build our network.

I got to travel to Brazil several times for work. I met some great people there. It was particularly awesome because early in the project when weekend work wasn't a must, we got to do some company-organized activities exploring different places in Brazil. Who knew there really is a place called Ubatuba! In Brazil I learned that words really do hold power. The word *ordinary*, for example, is not a word to use lightly. Until talking to the people I worked closely with there, I never thought twice about telling someone that I live in an ordinary house or have just an ordinary life with my ordinary family. In the United States, *ordinary* doesn't hold a derogatory connotation. In Brazil (and I learned later that the same is true in other Latin American countries) the word *ordinary* has the connotation that whatever is referred to as ordinary is somehow less than or of lower quality. By remembering this later, commenting on it with co-workers who were from other Latin American countries and listening to them, I was able to create the networks internally that mean I can connect with someone who remembers that I'm willing to listen, make mistakes, and learn from them.

I also learned that it is important to talk to people in your host country, but it is just as important to listen to them. By listening, and really hearing them, I learned that you don't have to be afraid to walk down the street in the bigger cities if you walk like you mean it and don't walk like a tourist. I am happy to say that I didn't heed the advice of our group leader on our business trips to Brazil. We were told often that you never ever left the hotel alone, you always traveled with a travel buddy and never frequent any of the stores around the hotel if at all possible. Rather than stricktly heeding the dire warnings, I took my room key, my phone and just a little spending money and went on small (only a few blocks in any direction) adventures. Not once was I mugged. If you walk like the people around you and you take care not to advertise that you are from elsewhere, people tend to leave you alone. In this particular instance, they also, unfortunately, assumed that I spoke Portuguese; however, a self-deprecating smile and a little quick Google Translate helped with that situation. If you keep your senses about you and your sense of humor, you can learn an amazing amount about wherever you are (foreign and domestic).

Regardless of where you are, with what group you are communicating, or with what media you are communicating, it's important to listen to hear and understand, not just to mark time until it's your turn to talk. If you listen or read to understand, it is far easier to convey your ideas when the time comes to do so.

It's important to understand the way other people perceive your listening and your attention. Know your audience. While I know that I can listen quite well in a meeting or a discussion while taking notes (I've been known to write entire programs in a meeting while following every word and injecting required input in the right places without having my actual attention wavering), I know that with certain people I am required to not take notes even on the discussion at hand because the person with whom I'm meeting sees that as disrespect. By understanding the needs of the people you're talking with, you can leave them feeling better about the conversation.

Think you don't already tailor your communication to certain situations? Think about how you talk when you are out with friends. Is that the way you talk when you are around young kids? Do you talk to your boss the way you talk to an elderly neighbor? Do you talk to your children or the children you encounter in the same way that you talk to your boss? Everyone already has some level of cultural communication awareness.

Now, we just need to expand how we think.

Key Takeaways and Lessons Learned

In this chapter, you learned that differences between cultures are not only those that cross national or international borders. You saw examples of times when being able to communicate effectively (hearing as well as speaking) has a monetary impact. Other times it simply makes a difference to our reputation or our ability to reach out to the network of people who we have communicated effectively with in the past.

By taking the time to learn a few key words or a few simple customs, we can prove ourselves as people who are good to work with. Building the trust that other people have in us, and that we can have in others, will make our work life more enjoyable and profitable.

References for Further Reading

Meyer, Erin. *The Culture Map (INTL ED): Decoding How People Think, Lead, and Get Things Done Across Cultures*. PublicAffairs, 2016.

Molinsky, Andy. *Global Dexterity: How to Adapt Your Behavior Across Cultures without Losing Yourself in the Process*. Harvard Business Review Press, 2013.

CHAPTER 2

Communication Is Culture

Just as every culture has its own unwritten rules that govern it, inside every culture there are similar unwritten rules that govern the communication endemic to that culture. Some of the rules are obscure and difficult to understand or learn, while others (the ones that usually make the biggest impact) simply take paying attention and putting some effort into learning. In this chapter, you will learn how different global cultures view communication and how it differs from what you might be comfortable with. We will take what we learned in chapter 1 a bit further and more specific. While most of us have our own concept of what communication is, it is usually bigger than what we think.

If you can expand your concept of what culture is, you can expand your idea of how to better to communicate with all of the people you come into contact with. Never let yourself box your brain in, whether it is in technology or communication.

Going Global

Businesses are becoming more and more global every day. Communicating in a global organization or with a global organization is as much an art as a science. In this chapter, we will look at some of the nuances of communicating globally, regardless of what country you are

© April Wells 2018
A. Wells, *The Tech Professional's Guide to Communicating in a Global Workplace*,
https://doi.org/10.1007/978-1-4842-3471-6_2

from, what country the people you are communicating with are from or in, and what cultures are involved.

Probably the most logical place to start talking about communicating across cultures is with what many people think of as the biggest cultural differences—There are those differences that exist between people who are from different geographical areas, for example France and Japan or the United States and Sweeden. It's not necessarily the people you work with every day who may cause you angst but people who are physically and geographically dispersed. While these cultural differences are not necessarily bigger than the differences between people who live in the same city or even neighborhood. Language is likely the biggest hurdle in many people's minds when dealing with communicating with these different cultures. If we remove l anguage difference from the equation it is easy to see that, while there are differnces, those differences aren't nearly as huge as our minds make them.

Isn't Global What It's All About Anyway?

Many people, when considering cultures and the idea of communicating across cultures, think primarily about living in one country and communicating with someone in another country. This is a valid view of the idea and one of the biggest places where people have issues with communication. It is particularly true when dealing with the differences in language.

Without a bit of an understanding about a generalized way that people interact in different countries, it is easy to slip into talking to everyone you deal with in the same way you deal with people who you work with every day. Oftentimes this works well; however, there are times when this creates issues in communication.

Lewis Model of Culture

When I was first starting to really think about the difference in the way people communicate, and more to the point, the way people think about words, I was in a conference session about working internationally and implementing Oracle E-Business Suite internationally. In 2016, there was a presentation at the Collaborate 16 conference in Las Vegas, Nevada, discussing how the differences in culture and in the way different cultures think about or react to the words that are used to describe ideas and new technologies in a project is far different from the way the same cultures feel about the technology that is actually being introduced to their daily work schedule. In fact, the way that people in one country think about words can be markedly different from the way that you think about words and by having a better understanding of what those word differences mean to all parties in discussions the transition into new ways of doing their jobs can be made much more elegant. The presenter suggested that the Lewis model of culture is a reasonably accurate way to look at the differences in the cultures of different countries and the way those differences can impede or assist in making projects or ordinary interactions better.

Richard D. Lewis has written several books on global culture[1,2] that deal in great depth with culture and cultural differences. While the topic of communication is covered, it is somewhat limited; however, the *When Teams Collide* book does provide insight into how different cultures communicate in a team setting.

Figure 2-1 shows my personalized adaptation of one of the most commonly referenced graphical representations of the Lewis model. I narrowed the picture down to just the countries that most closely represented the ones I've dealt with.

---

[1]Lewis, Richard D. *When Cultures Collide: Leading Across Cultures*, 3rd Edition. Nicholas Brealey Publishing, 2005.

[2]Lewis, Richard D. *When Teams Collide: Managing the International Team Successfully*. Nicholas Brealey Publishing, 2012.

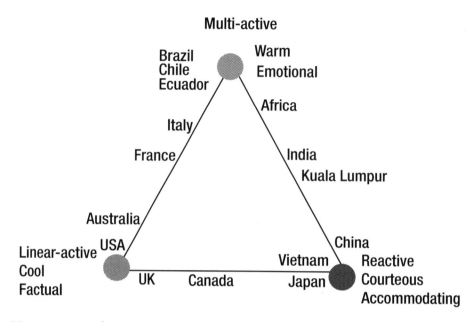

Figure 2-1. *The condensed Lewis model*

If you want to see the entire graphic, I suggest heading to one of the web sites mentioned at the end of this chapter that present the whole picture. The website `https://www.crossculture.com/about-us/the-model` is a good place to start.

It's interesting to look at where different countries lie on the sides of the triangle and to consider what the location and the implications mean to us. Lewis suggests that there are three basic culture types (multi-active, reactive, and linear-active) and that there are basic communication styles associated with those culture types.

People in Germany, for example, are linear-active and tend to be frank and direct while talking and listening in equal degrees. German people value truth before diplomacy, tend to talk in turns, and tolerate some degree of silence.

Compare this with the people in China or other Asian countries, the reactive cultures, and you will notice that the culture is indirect and cautious. Diplomacy is valued higher than truth, there are few confrontations, and they rarely if ever interrupt. People in the reactive countries listen most of the time and enjoy sharing contemplative silences.

Brazil and other South American and Mexican cultures are considered by Lewis to be multi-active. People who are from multi-active cultures tend to be indirect, often interrupt, work better if they can talk most the time, and tend to display rather than conceal feelings. Multi-active cultures tend to be able to talk over each other while maintaining an accurate understanding of everything that is going on, and they have a harder time tolerating contemplative silences.

This model was developed through extensive analysis of data gleaned from tens of thousands of executives in dozens of nationalities and countries, and the conclusions arrived at through the information are interesting and valuable to consider. It doesn't, however, consider the differences that occur in subcultures that occur within each and these overreaching cultures, such as the culture of accounting or the culture of marketing or the culture of technologists. The fact that most of us communicate via e-mail and instant messaging on a regular basis can often add complexity and interesting inconsistencies to the cultural paradigm without anyone involved being aware.

What I took away most from the discussion on this model was that people from more like cultures, because they are more apt to behave similarly, are more likely to communicate more similarly. This is not to say that they speak the same language because, obviously, a person from Sub-Saharan Africa isn't likely to natively speak the same language as someone from Brazil or Chile, but their style of communicating is more apt to be similar.

What you can take away from this model is an understanding of how to better understand the people who you are sitting with in a meeting or who you are helping with an issue. By understanding better the way someone else might be thinking and responding, you can better build the systems and implement the solutions that will meet the need that is spoken and unspoken.

Geert Hofstede

Another interesting academic who studies culture, not only as it applies to national cultures but also as it applies to business and work, is Geert Hofstede. His studies center around, primarily, internal organizational cultures in different international locations. There are, in Hofstede's model, six dimensions in a nation's culture.[3]

- *Collectivism versus individualism*: Do you feel that you are independent (individualism) and are encouraged to make your own choices and decisions? Or are you interdependent (collectivism) and you make your decisions as they apply to the station that you hold in life, as it pertains to your daily life? Typically, the model suggests, people in the United States are on the individualism end of the spectrum, and people in Asia are more on the collectivism end.

- *Power distance*: A power distance refers, in the Geert Hofstede model, to whether people who are less powerful think that the more powerful people are connected or disconnected from them and their situation in the society. In a large culture with a larger power distance acceptance, people believe completely that the leaders are disconnected from their issues and problems and that it is as it should be.

- *Femininity versus masculinity*: Despite the name, this doesn't refer to the number of men and women or even to the roles that men and women play in society. This refers to the way that force is exerted and accepted.

---

[3]http://geerthofstede.com/culture-geert-hofstede-gert-jan-hofstede/6d-model-of-national-culture/

If you are in a highly masculine culture, getting ahead and excelling are vital regardless of the gender of the individuals. In a predominantly feminine culture, competition is not critical to individuals within the culture; there is more acceptance and understanding toward not only the leadership and strong individuals but the less powerful groups and individuals.

- *Uncertainty avoidance*: If you are in a culture that is uncertainty tolerant, you are not anxious when it comes to change. This is not necessarily the same as being risk tolerant or risk averse, but because with change there is risk, they often tend to go hand in hand. As a member of an uncertainty-intolerant culture, you are likely to be more tied to rituals and are likely uneasy when change is introduced.

- *Time orientation*: Cultures focused on the long term have a belief that the world is always in flux and that preparing for the future always needs to be uppermost in the minds of the members of the society. If your culture is focused on the short term, you are more apt to believe that the world is as it has always been and maintaining this focus on keeping things as they are and as they have always been is the way to live not only today but to prepare for the future. Russia, according to `http://geerthofstede.com/culture-geert-hofstede-gert-jan-hofstede/6d-model-of-national-culture`, is on the long-term orientation end of the spectrum, and people in Libya and Albania tend to be on the short-term orientation end.

- *Indulgence*: If you are a member of an indulgent culture, your belief is that it is important to be free, to follow your instincts and impulses, and to be less focused on duty. Contrary to this, a culture that is more restrained and less indulgent believes there is a higher concept that life is hard, that duty is predominant in the culture, and that freedom (personal as well as societal) is less importance. It should not be surprising that North, South, and Central America are on the more indulgent end of the spectrum. Russia and Asia, on the other hand, tend to be on the more restrained end.

The Hofstede model, as it applies to corporations, suggests that there are eight dimensions to an organization's culture. The most measurable are the following:

- *Means versus goals oriented*: In a means-oriented organization, people concentrate on how the work is done, and in a goal-oriented organization, they typically are more focused on the internal goals and what those goals are and consider a variety of ways to accomplish them. Means-oriented organizations typically tend to avoid risks, while goal-oriented organizations are often less risk averse.

- *Internally versus externally driven*: In an internally oriented organization, people focus on business ethics and honesty to meet not only a customer's needs but societies' needs as well. People in externally oriented organizations focus more on the results of meeting the customer's needs and are more pragmatic rather than focusing on ethics.

- *Easygoing versus strict work discipline*: While easygoing organizations sound like they might be more fun to work in, the lack of internal structure and control that typifies these organizations would likely make for a stressful environment if easygoing were to be taken to the extreme. In a strict work discipline organization, people tend to be more punctual and serious about their work, and their organization's focus is less on relaxed predictability and more on cost and corporate awareness.

- *Local versus professional*: When you're in a local organization, you typically identify with the boss or the team/division/unit where you work, as opposed to a professional organization where you identify with your profession, your title, or the content of your job.

- *Open versus closed*: In an open organizational culture, newcomers and "outsiders" easily feel welcome and are accepted into the culture; a closed culture tends to exclude people who are not a member of the team. Closed cultures tend to resemble cliques.

- *Employee versus work oriented*: If you work in an organization that is employee oriented, you feel like your personal problems and work-life balance are taken more into account, as if the organization takes responsibility for your well-being. In the case of an employee-oriented organization, the work or the job typically takes a backseat to the employee. However, if you work for a work-oriented organization, there is a not so subtle emphasis on performance, and the job takes priority over the employee's needs. In an organization at the far end of the work-oriented spectrum, there are often issues with stress and employee burnout.

It is interesting to consider the differences in national culture with respect to the people living and working in any given country, but it is more important for an organization and the people in the organization to understand how their organizational culture fits, or doesn't fit, with respect to the country they are working in.

With the increasingly global nature of business, living in a country where individualism is high, where there is the expectation that uncertainty is not only tolerated but expected, and where personal freedoms are likewise accepted and expected while operating in a country where uncertainty tends to make people anxious and where personal decisions and expectations of freedoms are contrary to the culture of the country and the collective workforce, there can be difficulties. Add in the likely differences in language and other differences, and there can be not only discomfort but also mistrust.

Therefore, it's important to understand the way that you communicate ("hearing" as well as "talking") and the way that the audience for your communication is apt to be understanding your message.

Traveling Abroad

Traveling abroad brings with it many interesting adventures and new sights, sounds, and tastes, and it brings interactions with people who you may not have had the chance to work with or talk to before. You can also find that working in different countries brings challenges. Language differences remain one of the biggest challenges that face people who are working in countries other than their own. If you can work to learn a few key words and prhases, that can take much of the language issue out of the equation. While you may still be left with some cultural differences, people will be more apt to help you learn your way through those. Those non-language differences are often still difficult, but the feeling of good will that arises when you come in with a basic understanding can ease much of the way.

If you are traveling for work, there may be a group of people traveling either together or at the same time. This eases some of the angst that you might feel. This isn't always the case, however. Sometimes you will be traveling alone, and you need to do your research ahead of time to make the travel and work experience easier.

Better yet, make friends with people who are local to the country where you're going. If you can make friends with your co-workers, you can learn much faster because they can make it fun. They will give you the best hints and tips on what not to say, what to say, where to go, and where to avoid.

Understanding Holidays When Traveling

It's not uncommon to have a project in another country and when your plane lands you find that the plant where you are supposed to be working for the day has closed, with no one there to let you in or to assist in the project. It turns out there is a holiday and you didn't realize or were not informed. It also turns out that there isn't anywhere to get anything to eat except room service in the hotel or in the coffee shop in the lobby. While this isn't an insurmountable challenge, it is a challenge and can start your trip off on a difficult foot.

What happens when you are on a project in Brazil on their Mother's Day? You don't think about it much, right? Mother's Day is a great day to spend time with your mom no matter where you are, right? What you might not realize is that Brazil has a tradition of allowing criminals in the prison system a day of vacation so they can visit their mothers (or their wives as the mothers of their children) on Mother's Day. These prisoners, most of whom return after the day off, are likewise out where you would expect regular people and visitors to Brazil to be. Some of these prisoners are likely to take advantage of the opportunity that presents itself from unsuspecting or unknowing victims. By communicating well with your local counterparts, it is far more likely that you will not find yourself the victim of a crime of convenience.

Use Technology To Help You With Language Differences

While I was traveling with my family internationally, I learned more than once that a few words in a person's native tongue (even if they are not pronounced perfectly) can make a world of difference in the way that people perceive you. And as cliché as it might seem, some of the most welcome words that a person can hear are what we learned as kids as the "magic words" such as *please* and *thank you*. These along with *hello* and *good-bye* are all words that people love to hear in their own language, and it doesn't take long to be able to learn just that many words.

In fact, there are many smartphone apps that can translate languages for you. Even if you have to invest in a paid app, you will likely find it a good investment. You might not be comfortable with pronunciation, but showing someone the word or phrase you're struggling with can make for both a learning experience and a humorous anecdote later.

Don't expect perfection from yourself. No one expects it from you. People are usually happy that you are trying and will usually meet you more than halfway if they believe you are making an honest effort.

Transportation

If you are lucky enough to have your company (or whoever you are traveling with) organize your travel details for you, then this may not apply to you. If you, however, are like the majority of the people traveling in a different country, you may find yourself facing issues with local transportation.

Finding out the reality of transportation where you are going could be the most beneficial communication you can have. In China, for example, many of the taxi cabs are regulated by the government and are only permitted to charge the prescribed amount regardless of whether you are from China or you are working there or you are a tourist. If you don't know to watch for the license plate information that lets you know that the cab in question is licensed with the government, you may be amazed to see the meter spinning so fast that you can't even see the numbers racking up for the cost for the trip. A trip that would cost $10 US might end up costing $75 or $80 if you choose an unregulated taxi.

Another thing to be aware of when you are traveling overseas is the difference in traffic patterns. If you are from the United States, for example, it is important that you remain aware that when crossing the streets in London you need to look left first to make sure that nothing is coming on their correct side of the road that could take you by surprise. London is good at communicating with visitors; they paint in bold lettering on the curbs to look both ways to be sure that pedestrians are safe.

It's important to remember that communication can take many different forms, and it is equally as important to remember that it is up to every person to understand the communication that is coming their way even if it is in a form that they don't know to expect.

But What to Do Every Day?

But what does all of this mean to you in your everyday work life?

Whether you realize it or not, you deal with the global community on nearly a daily basis. Whether you work for an international, multinational, or global company like Walmart, Disney or Oracle, or you work for a company that is solely within one country like In and Out Burger or Joe's Coffee, you are likely dealing with global communication without even realizing it.

Think this is an overstatement?

It's not.

When you open a trouble ticket with a vendor, you may be dealing with a call center anywhere in the world. When you open a critical trouble ticket with a big vendor (think Oracle or Microsoft or VMware), you are almost assuredly working with someone in another country at least part of the time.

But work aside, think about buying your coffee, ordering lunch, going to a class at a community college, or going to the doctor's office. It doesn't matter how well people speak English; many of the people you encounter are from countries all over the world, and you need to communicate well with them.

If you happen to be on a team that is traveling for business to another country, it is even more critical.

You don't have to be fluent in every language or be fluent in any but your own native language to be able to present a professional appearance and put others at ease when dealing with people on a global spectrum.

Tech Professionals, Particularly

While it's true that there are expatriates and an international presence in almost every line of business, it is particularly true of the IT world. Nearly every company of any size with an IT department has technologists working all over the globe and quite likely technologists located in many different countries. It is often easier for us to relate to each other because we share common technology, whereas, say, accountants have differing ways of handling their jobs; however, when you are working internationally, it's important to remember that technology may be common, but that doesn't make us all the same.

When I was in Ecuador, I had very little interaction with the local IT folks. I went to our conference room as soon as I got off the bus in the morning, stayed there until lunch, ate with the people from the plant at lunchtime in the cafeteria, went back to the conference room, and spent the remainder of my day there. The only interactions I had with people who were from Ecuador were outside of work. However, there I got to work with several technologists from Argentina and Chile. I was warned well in advance that I would be greeted in traditional Argentinian style with a hug and a cheek kiss.

My work in Brazil was very different than my work in Ecuador. In Brazil I worked closely with the people who were in the IT department. We worked closely together, we ate lunch together in the cafeteria, we spent time together, and through the project we became friends. I learned much more because of this close working relationship. I learned that Portuguese is not Spanish, although there are similarities. I learned that the cultural expectation there was that lunchtime was lunchtime; you take the time to not only eat lunch but go for a short stroll around the plant afterward. Your weekends (unless the project requires weekend work) are expected to be your own and that you spend them relaxing. Acknowledging that they shared the similar frustrations to those that I had (that the visiting technologists had) was the gateway to better understanding the culture.

Out and About

No matter where you go or for what reason, if you are out of the country, you are going to have to be out and about and dealing with people from your host country. Everyone eats. Everyone buys something. You may need to take a taxi or public transportation. You are likely to have to order something in a restaurant, check in to your hotel, or shop.

By learning just a few key phrases, you will navigate any global setting effectively. Many restaurants provide pictures on menus, and waiters usually smile good-naturedly when someone points to what they want for their meal. Shopkeepers, particularly in bigger cities, are adept at interacting with people who speak different languages. Prices are usually marked on merchandise, and computerized cash registers typically show the total for a purchase.

When you are not in bigger cities or when you are spending time shopping in a marketplace, sometimes not being able to understand numbers is less elegant, however. This is particularly true when you are in a place where haggling with the shopkeepers or sellers is either common, expected, or looked on as an adventure. It's important to remember that you can use many unique ways to communicate a sales transaction in cases like this. Every cell phone has a key pad with numbers on it. Calculators have number pads as well. If you are having trouble understanding the cost of something or you are engaged in good-natured haggling, using your cell phone's calculator feature can be handy. An iPhone or iPod could be used to haggle over a price if language stands in the way. Oh, and just a little hint... if you are haggling over price and you have reached the price you think is your top price, don't be afraid to walk away. I got a beautiful brass "singing bowl" in China this way from someone selling their wares in a street market. I reached $20 US haggling in Yuan, and that was my limit. The woman still shook her head no. When I walked away, she ran after me to accept.

Casual Contact

Not everyone you encounter with an international background is through work. Stereotypes aside, you are going to run into people with recent international backgrounds nearly every day while you are out and about. International students end up working in retail or food service, amusement park workers are often international workers, and (while it is cliché) often people who are giving taxi, Uber, or Lyft rides are likewise international. No matter where you go, you are going to encounter people whose nationality and native language are not the same as yours.

As you will learn in Chapter 6, it sometimes just takes a little thought in advance to make sure you aren't offending someone with your body language and gesturing inadvertently.

Handy Places to Gather Information

You should do a little advanced research (or look for some quick refreshers when you're deep in the middle of somewhere); there are many websites that have information about individual countries and how cultures in the country are different from other cultures.

For example, Everyculture.com (`www.everyculture.com/index.html`) gives you some interesting information on almost every international culture you want to consider. You can look up by country to see what differences there are. Similarly, you can find interesting information on `http://businessculture.org` and `www.cyborlink.com`. These sites have a slant toward business culture differences. While none of the available websites has an exhaustive list of countries, they do hit most of the bigger ones you're likely to travel to or be interested in the culture of. Each site is broken down into countries, regions, and resources.

Closer to Home

Think that dealing with a variety of cultures is relevant only when dealing internationally? Understanding that cultural differences, and by extension communication differences, occur in your own country, your own city, your own company, and your own neighborhood is important to your ability to communicate effectively every day.

Want to try a little social experiment? Take a cup of your favorite beverage and pull up a bench in one of the parks in a town near where you live. Leave your headphones off, even if they are in your ears. Better yet, leave them in your ears; this makes people think you can't hear them. Watch and listen to the way people talk and interact around you. Don't engage; just observe.

Are people talking in a different language from you? Do you hear accents? Are there differences in younger people talking versus older people? Is there a difference in the words people use? Parents talk differently to children than they do to their peers or their elders. There is a difference between casual conversations between friends, formal conversations between police officers and possible law offenders, and business acquaintances passing through the park over lunch. These are examples of different cultures, different modes, and different methods of communication.

Management

If you watch managers talk to each other and then you watch a manager talk with their direct reports (or even their indirect reports), you can easily see a difference in the way they talk and interact. To lead in any organization, managers must become adept at communication and adopt the culture of management. This is critical information if you want to advance your career into management. It's even more critical to understand when you are communicating with your manager.

While there are always cultural differences between people, when you are dealing with such differences between you and your boss, it's politically important to make note of those differences and quickly adapt. It's often more important to adapt your communication style to your boss's style than to follow your own style, even if it means missing the finer points of what was discussed, those that you might have captured had you been able to follow your own method.

If you are in a meeting, regardless of the number of attendees, your boss might find it necessary to see that you are actively engaged in watching the meeting slides or listening to the speaker at the expense of being able to recount later through notes what was covered in the meeting. By adapting to a manager's communication style and underlying culture, you show respect.

Management is its own culture. Managers have concerns that often they don't feel the need to communicate to their reports. They have stresses connected to the knowledge that they have that is wider than what their direct reports understand.

"The Business"

If you haven't noticed, the people in departments that IT people refer to as "the business" (finance, HR, accounting, for example) have their own way of talking to each other. It's easy to get caught up in the differences, and we will look at many of the differences in Chapter 6, but until then, remember that every subculture inside of the overarching corporate culture has its own language, its own grammar, and its own meaning for words. While you still likely speak the same language when you talk to each other, you might be drawing entirely different conclusions and meaning from the words you are using. We will look at many of the ways that the way words are used in different departments can lead to misunderstanding in chapter 5.

While, as tech professionals, we have the business's interest in mind regardless of what part we play in the organization, we also tend to have a narrow view on different aspects of the company. We may work more closely with accounting than with HR, and for that reason it might be easier to see the accounting side of the overall business; we may not even understand to a great deal much about business outside of our own corner of technology. We do, however, need to be able to communicate intelligently with any of the departments that we come into contact with.

Different cultures have different slang and different acronyms that they use freely with people in similar cultures in the organization. Technologists certainly have our own that we use and assume that people simply must understand. This is not always the case. In Chapter 5 I'll talk in greater depth about the slang that different business cultures use and how to keep in mind what the differences mean in communicating between the different business cultures.

Teammates

We work as tech professionals. This means that we likely work with international co-workers. We speak the same language, for the most part, although sometimes we must listen carefully to understand when dealing with heavy accents from different countries or from different parts of the country we call home.

People have different genders, differing religion, differing sexual orientation, and different familial backgrounds. There are people on our teams who have their sights set on management or who are looking for opportunities outside of the organization. Because people are different and because people think differently depending on where they are in their lives, their culture and their communication will differ because of it. It's important when you choose to communicate with your teammates that you consider these differences and the idiosyncrasies.

Being able to communicate well with your teammates is important to the effectiveness of the team and the success of any project undertaken by the team. Team culture changes depending on the members of the team and the purpose for which the team was created. Sometimes communication at the team level means scheduling meetings and making sure you show up on time for the ones you are invited to. If your team crosses departments and has been created for a project, then effective and timely communication is even more important. Without timely communication of roadblocks and hurdles, members of the team from other departments could be surprised when they find out that they are required to put in extra hours or that timelines have slipped.

Multigenerational Communication

Because teams, groups, companies, and society consist of people at all stages of their careers and their lives, working and talking across the cultures with various generations is also, at times, a challenge. It's easy to fall into thinking about stereotypes when dealing with people of different generations even within your own culture. Avoid that. People from different age groups bring different knowledge and perspectives, and by listening to other viewpoints without rolling your eyes opens the lines of communication and will benefit everyone. It may be cliché, but you have two eyes and two ears and only one mouth. Listen and watch, with an eye to hearing and seeing and less to just waiting until it is your turn to talk. People in middle age and those approaching retirement likely have years of experience behind what they are saying, and younger people just starting their careers have a fresh eye to see things from a different perspective. Neither is right, and neither is wrong in any given situation. (It's not right, it's not wrong, and it's just different.) By hearing each other out, all generations can learn and provide the best solution to any problem the organization throws at them.

As you can see, there are many things that roll up into someone's culture. Keeping this in mind will make it easier to communicate with people regardless of what their culture is and how that culture differs from yours.

Differently Abled Communication

Another culture that you need to take into account is the culture of those who are differently abled. Not everyone you are going to work with or come into contact with is going to communicate in the same way you do. There is no need to feel uncomfortable with people who communicate differently. People are people no matter what they look like or how they communicate.

Many of us learned a smattering of American Sign Language when we were in school. The sign language alphabet comes in handy when you need to communicate simply with people who are deaf or hard of hearing. The sign language alphabet is simple to learn, and while it doesn't have the elegance and robustness of ASL proper, it is robust enough to facilitate communication when communication is necessary with people who can't hear your voice. Learn a few useful signs to add to your repertoire, and soon you will be conversing comfortably.

Are you doubting that even a few simple signs can make a difference? It may not mean that you will be the interpreter to the stars, but it can mean the difference between being uncomfortable in a situation and being able to handle a conversation with aplomb. Moreover, it can mean the difference between someone who you are talking to being incredibly uncomfortable and having that person leave with a smile on their face. Several years ago, while my family was at Disneyland, we went shopping. When we approached the cash register, the woman who was running the register was struggling to communicate without having to write notes to the people whom she was helping. She was embarrassed and frankly harried. Because my kids both took ASL as their foreign language in school (and if that doesn't tell you that the deaf community is a culture different from what you might understand, nothing will) and because I had been helping them learn, as a result I was able to communicate with a smile and thank her with the ASL sign for thank you in a way that not only she understood but made her smile. It didn't add to anyone's bottom line. It probably didn't have the lasting impact on her that it had on me and my kids, but for just a moment in her busy day, it made her smile.

As with spoken language differences, you don't need to be fluent in a language to start using the words you do know.

Key Takeaways and Lessons Learned

You started this chapter looking at what you might think of as communication and different ways that people communicate based on their particular culture, and you learned to expand your definition of *communication* to encompass much more. You looked at what communication is and the differences in what we think of as culture. By expanding your definition of *culture*, you can ease communication issues that might occur. Avoiding misunderstandings means that you don't have to make amends later, and this can save both time and energy as well as leave people with the understanding that you are aware of your surroundings and how to navigate there. Reputation and goodwill are priceless.

References for Further Reading

Looking for more information on cultures, cultural differences, and the world we live and work in? Here are a few places to start looking.

If you want to learn a little (who am I kidding, a lot) more about the Lewis model, a good place to start is at `https://www.crossculture.com/about-us/the-model/`.

In fact, I highly recommend this site and drilling down into more information on the different classifications. It will help you not only see other cultures in a different light but will allow you to see your own culture differently; it helped me see why some of the things in my daily life are the way they are.

For more on Geert Hofstede, visit `https://geert-hofstede.com/` and `https://www.hofstede-insights.com/product/compare-countries/`.

The latter site shows how countries compare to one another but more specifically what most countries have as their Geert Hofstede model characteristics.

Interested in learning a little, or a little more, sign language? There are apps out there (go figure, right?) that can help you learn American Sign Language (ASL) or British Sign Language (BSL), and most either are free or have a free version you can use.

While there are far more apps for iOS than there are for Android devices, helpful apps do exist for both operating systems. There are also many valuable Internet sites that can be used from any device.

Lifeprint (`www.lifeprint.com/`) has a robust (paid) iPhone/iPad app that lets you practice finger spelling (which will work for communication when you don't have a broad range of signs) called ASL: Fingerspelling. The website itself has a deep and broad offering of ways to learn to communicate with ASL.

ASL Dictionary by Software Studios has an app that is updated frequently that provides more than 5,000 words that you can start using almost immediately. Again, it is a paid app, but for the price you can't go wrong, and it is available on iOS as well as on Android.

Google Play provides apps that allow you to learn BSL because just as there are differences in British English and American English, there are similar differences between BSL and ASL.

Sign BSL on Google Play is a free app that teaches you (through video) on your Android mobile device.

Indian Sign Language (ISL) has its own app on Google Play from Talking Hands.

Prefer to learn ASL online? There is an online sign school at `https://www.signschool.com/welcome/` that you can work through, which even has a e-mail service that sends you a free sign every day to add to your conversational vocabulary.

Beginning lessons teach you how to greet people, introduce yourself, and ask other people their names. You start small and work your way up.

To find information on many countries and cultures, I suggest you visit the following locations:

`www.everyculture.com/index.html`

`http://businessculture.org`

`www.cyborlink.com`

CHAPTER 3

Women and Communication: Tales from the Trenches

I think there are some people who don't consider that women are a different culture. To some degree we are looked on as just another one of the guys. We are, however, not just one of the guys. If we were, communication for people in IT would be a little less of a challenge. While you may or may not consider that men and women have different cultures, it's a fact that we do. Even if boys and girls are raised in a family that tries to impart upon them that both girls and boys can achieve anything that they want, the fact is that no one is raised in a vacuum. Society imprints on boys and girls that they are different and provides them with behaviors that are expected.

Biology aside, it's important for women to understand how they are different from men, culturally as well as in the way that they communicate. Men should also consider how their culture is different than that of women; as a result, their method and manner of communication are also, likewise, different. By thinking about your strengths and the way you approach communication, it is possible for you to communicate more constructively.

41

© April Wells 2018
A. Wells, *The Tech Professional's Guide to Communicating in a Global Workplace*,
https://doi.org/10.1007/978-1-4842-3471-6_3

The differences between people of different countries or between different regions within the same country (for example, north versus south in the United States or North Korea versus South Korea) are considered to be *intercultural* differences. These, as I've discussed, are what people typically think of as cultural differences. The differences between people who live within one area are usually considered to be *intracultural* differences. These differences are usually factors such as generational differences, socioeconomic differences, or gender differences. While there are as many, if not more, differences between men in one country and women from another, in this chapter we are looking at the differences between males and females in the same general locale.

Looking at the culture of the United States, it's easy to see some marked differences. Men have traditionally tended to use stronger, more forceful language than women. They are typically raised to excel at sports, and they take this mind-set into the rest of their interactions in life. Men are taught to be strong and to strive to succeed often at all costs. Women, on the other hand, tend to use more "feeling" words in their interactions. They are usually raised to consider all aspects of an equation and find a solution in which everyone benefits and everyone can save face. These traits are usually divided by gender, but not always. Recall, however, from Chapter 2 that there are masculine traits and feminine traits that center on relationships and creating connections and are not necessarily attributable to gender. A masculine culture emphasizes goals, and aggressively chasing those goals is likewise not relegated just to males. Feminine cultures tend to value more the road to achieving the goal rather than the achievement itself. In this chapter, we will concentrate on the difference between males and females in within one culture.

We Aren't All That Different Really

While the premise of this chapter is that there are cultural differences that lead to communication differences, the truth is we really aren't that different. If you, a woman, were to look at your co-workers or your boss, you might stop and remember that we are really, even with all of our differences, all the same. He, over there, goes home at lunch to give his diabetic cat his insulin shots. She, a little to the left, has been with the company for more than two decades, has risen to middle management, and has learned to play the corporate culture game and still have a happy home life. See him, over there? He just handed in his resignation at the company because he found that he could no longer deal with the travel, long hours, or unexpectedness of his current job and decided to find a better balance. And what about her? Over there, on the right. She just learned that she has a serious illness (or that her partner or parent or child has a serious illness) and that life is short and has realized she needs to focus on different priorities. We all face challenges. We all make choices. We all have our own lives to lead. We are all human, and in that humanity we are all more similar than we are different. But there are differences, and that is why we are here.

Women Are Different

Wait, what? Women are different in terms of communication than their male counterparts? Women are different culturally and as a subculture within any global culture. They traditionally have been raised to not voice strong opinions. They are raised to be nurturers and caretakers even when they are also being raised to be feminists and understand that they can do anything they put their minds to. It is usually a mixed message. Men are encouraged to be aggressive and that the goal is the goal and that is where the focus needs to be. Women typically have a different way of thinking through problems and issues. The goal is always going to be the goal, but women often have a different cultural route of getting there.

It is important to remember that avoiding gender stereotypes (shoehorning people into a preconceived notion of expectations) based on their sexual identity or even their gender identity is no more or less OK than stereotyping people based on nationality, age, or sexual orientation is not okay. It's even more important to understand and remember that in many situations making generalizations can get you into trouble and sometimes is even legally actionable. Consider differences. Be mindful of yourself, but don't fall into stereotyping anyone—male, female, age, nationality, or anything else.

The different perspectives that women bring to society allow them to look at problems and challenges in different ways. People in most cultures have come far in breaking down gender roles and gender stereotypes, but even though stereotypes may or may not exist, differences still do.

It has been well publicized that women communicate differently than men. Recall the 1992 book *Men Are from Mars, Women Are from Venus* by John Gray where the different communication methods became a popular topic for discussion on the talk show circuit. Women often speak the same technological language as the men we work with, but the communication differences between women and men can sometimes still create communication issues.

Many studies have shown that women talk as a way to create relationships, or connections. They don't always use more words, as has been touted over the years by other studies, but they do use them differently. Women listen to the discussion and then oftentimes think it over before they try to posit a solution. Men, on the other hand, tend to listen to the discussion to get the basic details and to determine the solution even if there isn't an actual problem to solve.

As an example, there are times when my husband and I will talk after work. I will have had a truly stressful day, and I just want to talk it through. There is no problem that needs to be solved. The day is over, there is no going back through it, and there is nothing that can actually be done to change whatever the issue is that is bothering me. But for me (and for many women), talking through whatever it is helps me to figure out in my own head what it is that I'm struggling with.

My husband listens and hears, but he does what I've also seen many men do; he tries to figure out almost immediately how to fix the unfixable. It frustrates him when he realizes that it is outside of his power to fix some of the issues. He tries. He gives me suggestions (suggestions that I usually know anyway), but there is nothing he can really do but to listen.

I don't usually look for the solutions. I just need to talk it through. Once he came to terms with that fact, he quit getting frustrated. I believe there are many times that he actually just tunes me out while I talk it through.

Generalizations aside, logic has taught me that while all mammals have fur and all dogs are mammals and therefore all dogs are animals that have fur (if a, then b; if b, then c; and therefore if a, then c) logic doesn't dictate human behavior. Not all women need to talk things through, and not all men need to try to fix things. But studies have shown these tendencies do exist, albiet with exceptions on both sides.

Recall the earlier discussion on masculine versus feminine cultures and how masculine cultures (country, company, society) tend to focus on success (however they define success...typically by money and status, success, and winning in competition). Businesses, globally, are often built on the idea of making money and being successful (because no company sets out to lose money; they are in business because they want to be profitable). While masculine doesn't always equate to male, in many cultures often it does because these things are crucial to a masculine culture...to a man. Solutions and self-reliance are critical; they solve problems.

Feminine cultures traditionally are considered to be caring, supportive, and relationship oriented. They value discussion for the purpose of discussing and creating relationships. While solutions to actual problems are important, it is often just as important to talk through whatever is happening.

Keeping the differences in mind as you communicate between genders can help make progress overall.

Just because we are different, however, doesn't mean that we are less. If we are hired, our credentials are just as high as anyone else's in the same job class we are hired in to. One of the most irritating things to me, and to many women in IT, is when we are told, either through implication or outright, that we are only there because we are filling a quota or we are less favorable than the men we are working with.

One young woman, after graduating with a BS from a prestigious university, was hired into a very large corporation. She was told by her hiring manager that she was a priceless commodity. She was a woman (minority), and she was ethnically a minority. The hiring manager told her that by hiring her they filled two quotas in one fell swoop. The only thing that could have made it better is if they could have found a way for her to fulfill a disability—a trifecta. She told people about the opportunity this offered her, but she also said that it made her feel that her degree was to a great extent a waste because being told she was being hired because she filled two "quota" positions was demoralizing.

It's not typical that managers are quite as blunt as this. And while honesty is commendable from both men and women in the workplace, it is also important to remember the HR training many of us get every year that can keep awkward situations from arising.

It's not always easier once women get hired, though; more often it doesn't matter where you are in your career or what your acknowledged accomplishments are. Women often still face an attitude that we are. Not long ago, relatively speaking, I sat in a "war room" meeting where people were discussing the relative merits of one of the women who had just walked out of the room. The discussion included how much she brought to the meetings without even having to do anything or say anything; just by being there she brightened "everyone's" day, amid "good-humored" laughter and grins. In the same meeting, it was suggested that another woman who was troubleshooting an issue might want to send a message to one of the men she worked with to figure out what she was obviously not understanding.

It's easy to see how sometimes women can seem like they are more sensitive or reactionary than men; it's often because we have gotten used to having to be. Sometimes it's hard to curb your emotions at the door when you walk into what can sometimes feel like an antagonistic environment.

Don't Take It Personally

Women tend to have a reputation for being overly emotional. They are considered to take criticism, conflicts, and difficult conversations overly personally. While to some degree it is easy to see why women might feel angry or frustrated because the conflict is often overly personally, it is also important for women to understand that if they act on those feelings, they are doing little to further their case and are doing more to perpetuate stereotypes.

Where men seem to more easily brush off something someone says rather than to take it personally, women are more likely to focus on what they might have done differently and to be more emotional over a comment. They are less apt to think critically about direct or implied criticism and are therefore perceived to be overreacting. It's important to balance what you are actually hearing in a conversation rather than what you believe to be being implied.

This isn't always easy. We all spend nearly as much of our awake time at work or commuting to or from work. We are passionate about our jobs. Women are more emotional overall than men and therefore are more apt to take things that happen at work personally. It's often difficult to take the emotion out of the situation or to remove yourself from what you feel to be an emotionally charged situation to think through the situation and the implications.

Take a deep breath. Remove yourself from the situation if possible. Think through what has been written or said and think even more through your response. Don't dash off an angry e-mail. Don't say something that you might regret sooner rather than later.

Leverage What You Are Good At

While it is often frustrating to realize that, globally or at least in many places in the United States, women are viewed as being the ones with "soft skills"—they are the caretakers, the mothers, or the ones who make everyone break for lunch. While this is, as much as anything, a stereotype, stereotypes come from somewhere. People can either work hard to break them or work within their confines to make communication more elegant.

There has to be some irony in the fact that I am one of the earliest people to arrive at work. I work with my strengths, and I know that I am best in the morning. There was an Army commercial several years ago that suggested that people in the Army get more done before 9 a.m. than most people get done all day. The same is true for me. I know that I get more done before 9 a.m. than I get done the entire rest of the day because I'm a morning person and because by getting in early I avoid most of the distractions that are part of the remainder of the day.

There is a downside to this, however, because it also means that people expect the coffee pots to be filled and there to be cups and coffee in the cupboards when they get in. Typically, this is a valid expectation of me, not because I'm doing the caretaking thing but simply because I'm early and I really enjoy drinking coffee. If I wait until 9 or 10 a.m. to get a cup of coffee, the pots are nearly dry, and I simply get frustrated at the situation. If I'm off work or I happen to get my coffee at the coffee shop on the way in, usually people will seek me out to make sure everything is OK because the expectation is that coffee will be there.

Stereotypes come from somewhere, whether deliberate or inadvertent.

I can honestly say that there are many days when I look up from working on a particularly interesting problem to find that it is 2 or 3 p.m. Not only have I worked through lunch, but I have likely worked through meetings and not even noticed. I can also safely say that there have been times when I have made a point of suggesting that we break either to have lunch or to visit the restroom because things have gotten to a sticking point or because tensions are getting high. By voicing the obvious, sometimes met with grumbles and consternation, women on the team can find ways to break the tension, and everyone can come back to the table with a different mind-set and put the issues back into perspective.

I was once told that my boss had absolutely no faith in my being a productive member of his team. I admit that that was the one thing that made me go find employment elsewhere. When I tendered my resignation, I provided proof that I was told that "first thing in the morning, you need to be prepared to do X, Y, Z," and when I came in in the morning, those things had already been done by my boss. The exciting, challenging work was given to my male counterparts, and I was called repeatedly into my boss's office to proofread his e-mails so he didn't look bad. He leveraged something I was particularly good at but at the expense of allowing me to do other things that I was equally good at but that he enjoyed doing.

Never be afraid, if you get in a situation where you are being utilized primarily for your soft skills at the expense of your technological skills and you are not happy with the situation, to change the situation.

Studies have shown that men and women tend to focus differently on the same or similar situations. Men, as a general rule, tend to focus on one task almost completely and wall off activities from other tasks. Women, on the other hand, tend to be better at multitasking and working more with multiple pieces in parallel. This could be partially because women tend to also be more "big picture" oriented than men. By realizing and remembering that men are task oriented and focus on the immediate while women are big picture and parallel processing oriented, it becomes easier to tailor communication to these strengths.

There is not just anecdotal evidence of this. Studies have shown that women have more neurons in the language and hearing centers of their brains than men. Men's talents lie elsewhere.

Speak Up

Have you ever been in a meeting and noticed that the women in the room often tend to talk less than the men in the room? They often spend much of the meeting listening to the dialogue and hearing all sides of the conversation. When they do talk, it's often to gather more information rather than trying to jump to solutions to problems that might or might not exist. When they do talk, particularly when they use the same tone and language as their male counterparts, they are often perceived to be overly aggressive, confrontational, or even "bitchy."

Further, women in general tend to be reluctant to take credit for the things that they do. When talking about their accomplishments, they are more apt to phrase it as "we" did this or that rather than "I" did this or that. The tendency is even more pronounced when women are part of a mixed-gender group effort, suggests a study in *Personality and Social Psychology Bulletin*. The same reluctance is not apparently present when they are in women-only teams. Men, on the other hand, tend to rarely be reluctant to step up and take credit where they believe credit to be due. For that reason, men are also more apt to be recognized for their contributions in mixed-gender situations.

Not getting credit for contributions has been cited by people of both genders as a reason for lower morale and job satisfaction as well as a reason some have given for seeking other jobs. However, men are more apt to speak up about their personal part in a project or in remedying a problem, where women are more apt to speak in generalities. Men tend to speak more powerfully and are typically more "I" oriented, and women are more "we" oriented in speaking and tend to assure that the team is recognized often at their own detriment.

Meetings

While it is the case that there are situations where no input is required, expected, or tolerated, it is also the case that women tend not to speak up and provide input in meetings where such input is expected. Recall earlier that women's brains have more neurons in the listening center of the brain than men, so naturally it is likely that women will listen to all sides before weighing the information and making a suggestion. It is further cultural for us to be reluctant to speak up, and when we do, we tend to use less forceful words in our statements. We play down our knowledge in order to be more accepted and acceptable.

I'm not espousing talking simply to talk. For example, I would not even attempt to discuss accounting practices or automobile mechanics. Those are not my areas of strength and knowledge. Where my strengths are, however, I work hard to voice concerns when I know issues will occur.

It's hard to realize, however, that biases still exist in a large number of IT organizations, and the biases occur not only when men and women are communicating with each other but are also perpetuated by women with women (discussed later in the chapter).

My first job in IT was when I was newly hired full-time employee after being an intern. When my conversion to full-time was announced, one of the first comments I heard was "I'm so glad you're coming on board; now I won't have to make the coffee anymore." I learned early in my career that words make a lasting impression.

Skip forward several years, and I was working on a data warehouse project. In a meeting it was suggested that since Oracle will let you have 1,000 columns in a table, it should be okay to put all of the data into one table with nearly 1,000 columns so that we could avoid ever having to join tables to get data out. I pointed out that just because you can do something doesn't mean there is always justification to do it, and in many cases performance could be much worse with this design. I was told to shut up and that I didn't know what I was talking about and that they would ask one of my male co-workers for his opinion on the design.

Same company, different project: we were installing Oracle E-Business Suite. I worked all night long most nights patching and cloning and doing all of the maintenance things, and in the morning the business expert would come in to do setups. He would be nicely showered after sleeping and going to the gym and would walk into the server room and say, "Honey, go fetch me some coffee." Again with the coffee? My name isn't Honey, I am not a golden retriever, and I do not fetch outside of a cursor. If you want coffee, get yourself coffee.

Skipping ahead again: I was working a database application install issue, and we were having issues. The error, repeatedly said a table, didn't exist. When I tried to explain (gently at first, then more adamantly, and finally sarcastically I'm afraid) that it was a database error and that we had likely missed a step somewhere and maybe we should stop and go back and check, I was told the only reason I was working on the install was that they couldn't get any other more qualified DBA. I was told that Fred didn't have the problem last time he did the install. Fred did an "ls" at the command prompt. Maybe I should try doing an "ls" to see if that would fix it, and when it didn't, I was asked if I was sure I did an "ls" the right way. Is there a wrong way? And how exactly is listing the values in a directory going to fix an issue with the install? Finally, one of the men (a technofunctional team member) on the WebEx meeting suggested that maybe we missed something earlier and we should step through it again; all of a sudden that was an incredibly good idea. When I pointed out that I had made that suggestion more than a half-dozen times, I was told that I should stop trying to find blame and just shut up so we could get this installation done.

As I earlier suggested, these are examples of why women tend to not speak up or why we feel it is better to just pretend that we have no ideas of our very own and to work in silence in the background to make sure that projects succeed while keeping the attention off of ourselves. This is not the way it should be, and we, as women, need to stop doing it. Eventually, if we voice our ideas and suggestions in a calm and professional manner, someone will listen. Someone will pay attention, and even if they later suggest the same thing before it is done, at least the idea will be heard.

With Your Boss

I'm not certain if it a personality trait or cultural, but I know that for me, and for some other women I know, it is difficult to stand up to a boss when we believe we are being unfairly judged. I know that, for me, it is easier to internalize criticism and to second-guess myself where it appears that men simply assert themselves and expound and explain their positions.

It's important that you take the time to learn your boss's personality and how he or she prefers interactions to be handled. Some, if they have come up through the ranks of technologists, prefer to have as many interactions as possible done electronically, preferably through e-mail where there is a way to go back and check details. Others would rather handle everything face to face. Sometimes it's OK to take notes while you are discussing things with your boss; other times it is only OK if they take notes and you pay strict attention.

It can be particularly difficult for an active learner to become passive in an attempt to present the correct impression to the people they are working with. This is particularly difficult for me because I listen and learn better if I can be actively engaged in the process. I take notes so I don't forget what is going on or what is being said. When I need to meet with someone who has a higher official position who prefers that I not take notes, I've resorted to audio recording the meetings so I can go back later and take a more active part in the meeting virtually.

Women much more often take the criticism in meetings with people above them in the power structure of an organization personally and often react emotionally rather than clinically and logically. This is usually not the case when dealing with people on the same organizational level as we are. By reacting emotionally, however, we lose credibility not only from our bosses but from anyone who is witness to the outburst; further, we foster the idea that we are stereotypical women and can't be taken seriously.

Giving and Receiving Feedback

Feedback tends to be, on average, more negative than positive in the workplace. Feedback is given as a means to provide someone with the tools that will allow them to improve in their performance. By listening to and heeding feedback, it is possible not only to improve your daily work but to improve your chances of being promoted and getting that raise.

Studies in World Economic Forum (Women in the Workplace 2016) have shown that there is a disparity in both quality and quantity of feedback given to women and that given to their male counterparts. While managers believe that they give feedback to their men and women employees equally, women suggest that they seek feedback but feel that they receive the really honest hard feedback far less often than the men they work with.

The 2016 study shows that this is not just a perception but is a reality. They may or may not get some feedback, but they don't get the hard feedback—the really useful feedback—because the people giving the feedback are worried that the feedback will sound mean or hurtful, and they do not want to hurt the feelings of the women they are evaluating. Rather, they provide somewhat more vague feedback and allow women to infer what they should do with it, or they provide what amounts to simply negative and personal feedback rather than constructive feedback.

This is a disservice in communication to the woman getting the less than effective feedback, but it is also detrimental to the supervisor and to the company because they are going to end up with a less effective employee.

Look at the feedback. Look at the person providing the feedback. Do you entirely trust the motives in the feedback they are providing? Are they in the official capacity of providing you the feedback? Are there valid points in the feedback? Take those points and evaluate how you can use the feedback to make yourself better.

Are you responsible for providing feedback to women? Are you a woman responsible for providing feedback? Think about how you are phrasing your feedback and whether the feedback you are providing is constructive. Understand how different cultures or different genders accept and understand the feedback you are providing. Provide feedback as it pertains to an individual, particularly when you are talking to your female team members. Men typically hear reference to their impact on business outcomes or personal technological expertise; women tend to either hear how they are too aggressive (even when compared exactly equally to the men they are working with) or that they contributed to the team rather than they were personally impactful.

Be honest and don't try to be overly nice when providing feedback to women, even fellow women, on your teams. Men tend to be told in plain uncertain terms what they are doing wrong and what they are doing right. If you do, you are doing them a disservice. If you are too nice or set your expectations too low for women on your team because you are trying to be nice or cut them a break, you are setting them up later for failure and, worse, making us feel like we can't take the truth that you are more than willing to give male co-workers.

By focusing on behavior and outcomes, words, and intentions, rather than personality or by taking it personally, it is much easier to deal with feedback to all team members.

Don't Question Suggestions

It's easy for us to fall into the trap of questioning and second-guessing when people give us the leeway to do or not do things based on our best judgment. It's particularly difficult for women to not fall into the trap of trying to do more and more with no other purpose than to, in our own minds, simply keep up with our male counterparts.

If a co-worker offers to help because he has free cycles, be willing to take him up on it. If your boss offers to let you take a pass on a meeting, don't ask if she's sure and keep offering to go anyway. Take the time to focus on other aspects of your career or on a particularly interesting project. And if someone whose opinion you trust suggests an alternative to an issue you're working on when you're talking together one on one, make note of it and act on the suggestion when you get the chance.

It's easy to fall into the trap of thinking people might have an ulterior motive for making such offers or for giving you unsolicited advice, but that is rarely the case. Further, it's even easier to take such things personally when it's not meant to be. It may be difficult to not internalize when your supervisor tells you that he has no faith in your ability to be a productive member of his team, but even something phrased in such a blunt and disrespectful manner should not leave you unable to take the overly critical comments and turn them around to make yourself a more productive member of your team.

Brand Yourself

Men have a tendency to be more willing than women to toot their own horn publicly. Women tend to play down some of the things that make them stand out. There are some amazingly talented women who hide their talents rather than showcasing them and making themselves known for their strengths. They tend to worry that people will think that they are showing off or bragging.

Branding yourself online is the way you showcase yourself, showcase your talents, and show off your personality. We, as women, have frequently been told that we need to not show off because it makes us intimidating or less easy to work with, but this is just as often an excuse.

Online

Develop an online presence. Look around at the technology blogs, Twitter feeds, and discussion group threads and notice that most of the online presences are the men we work with. Men ask the questions and answer the questions. Men write about what they have learned and what they have stumbled across. Even when they are engaged in active discussions or lively arguments, they continue to post, they continue to tell other people, and they continue to discuss. Women are apt to read the information extensively but are not as apt to be out there and write about the technology. They know. They understand, but they don't usually write about it.

There are, of course, exceptions to the suggestion that women are less apt to put themselves "out there" with their online brand. The exceptions are wonderful to read and to make note of.

Heli Helskyaho (Heli from Finland) was the speaker at the first Women in Technology (WIT) luncheon that I attended at Collaborate in Las Vegas. She is active on Twitter, Facebook, and LinkedIn and has a very active blog presence. Her topic at the WIT lunch was on not being afraid to say yes.

Another, Kellyn Pot'Vin-Gorman (DBA Kevlar), has a prolific online presence, is active on social media, and leverages her own brand.

It is not that there are not incredibly successful and talented women in IT, but the online presence of women seems to be lacking when compared to the male counterparts.

If you want to have a constructive online presence, be easy to contact. Answer questions in discussions, respond to Twitter and Facebook posts, and join groups or follow people who have interests similar to your own. In that way, you can gain insight and provide your own expert advice wherever you can. Have a blog? If not, you might want to get one. If you do, answer questions or comments and provide links to other blogs that interest you. Create a positive online presence that will leave people with the impression of you that brings you to mind in constructive situations. And never do anything that is counter to your values. Be yourself and be genuine. People will remember you. You might attract some ugly attention (bullies, trolls), but you will gain a reputation for what you know and what you bring to the table.

Join groups on Facebook and LinkedIn; join Women In Technology groups to gain support and insight from fellow women technologists. It's amazing how even after several years of silence in industry discussion groups, I still run into people who recognize my name and strike up conversations about a litany of topics. Until recently, I hadn't realized that it mattered when I was answering questions and making suggestions. I was often left with the feeling that the information I was imparting to the conversation was trivial or of less value and my assumption (accurate or not) was that I was viewed as lacking because of my gender. Like if I had obfuscated my name it might have met with more discussion. I always (and I think women do this to a far greater extent than men) felt like I was just me and not anything like <insert whatever well-known male in the industry>, but it's been proven more often than I care to realize that just the opposite is true. I have been looked to bor my value as an "expert" or at least someone who can provide relevant valuable advice. Don't underestimate your impact. It's never important the gender of the person sharing information or knowledge only that the knowledge is shared.

Think about starting a blog. Seriously consider it. It only takes a bit of time, and it's a good way to share your findings and insight. You might not consider yourself an expert, but if you start writing about what you are discovering or what you know, you will discover that you might not be the most knowledgeable in every aspect of your subject, but you are going to be more knowledgeable than someone who finds your blog and discovers how helpful it is. This can help you in your career now or in the future. It can also help you make contacts with other people who are more knowledgeable than you, and you can gain your own knowledge and reputation. Decide on what you want to focus on. Are you a programmer? A system administrator? A DBA? There are very reputable low-cost avenues you can follow to make yourself known. Register your own name as your domain name; for less than $50 a year you can create a blog, register your domain, and start building your following.

Talk Person to Person

You need to consider your branding as much when you are face to face as you do when you are online. Remember the adage that you have ten seconds (some say three) to make a lasting impression on people you meet. You need to use those precious seconds to the best of your advantage. You never know if the person you are meeting is going to be the key person in your future, and leaving them with the wrong impression of you could have very lasting consequences.

Your Elevator Pitch

Men I've worked with tend to have a well-thought-out elevator pitch. I don't, personally, know many women where I've worked who have given theirs much thought. Most, when asked, have a general idea of their accomplishments and topics to discuss but don't have a polished speech ready. In fact, I really hadn't given mine any consideration until I went to present a paper at a conference. When I started to talk to people on the vendor floor, I didn't really know what to say when they asked me who I am, what my talk was about, and what I do. Having a 30- or 60-second speech prerecorded in your head that can answer the relevant questions really helps. You want to be careful about using jargon that is understandable or relevant to only a narrow group of people. Be as clear and succinct as possible so anyone at any level of expertise can understand what you are trying to convey.

I've always had a problem with the notion of it being an elevator pitch since I'm rarely in the elevator with anyone where I work and since no one tends to strike up conversations with me when I am. More precisely, consider it your 30-second infomercial on you. What would you want to know about someone who you would look at for a new position, for information in a unique situation, or to give you advice somewhere down the line in your career? Craft it in such a way to answer those situations.

Your elevator pitch is a way to give yourself confidence in talking to upper management, it can be useful in getting your name in front of people who can help you with your career, and it can help you get name recognition elsewhere as well. I've never actually been in an elevator with anyone who appeared to not be listening to music on their phone, who was involved in a discussion when they entered the elevator, or who wasn't someone with whom I was already acquainted. That's not to say the elevator pitch is not important. By having, at the ready, some of your own accomplishments, again recalling that women tend to focus on the "we" rather than the "I," you can be more ready to engage in small talk in conference or class situations and can help build your own network.

Showcase Your Accomplishments

Make sure that you have a ready set of "what I can do" information at your fingertips. We all dread the annual review process where we have to make a conscious and concerted effort to go back over our accomplishments of the past year and usually have to spend time pouring through our notes and memories of what we did for the company. But it is important to you, as a woman in IT, to be able to pull out from your memory the information on what you have accomplished in your career.

I went to a Women in Technology luncheon a couple of years ago, and it struck me, early in the presentation, that the presenter really had her ducks in a row. She had multiple slides on what she had done in her career. She showed milestones that were impactful on her life, that were impactful to her career, and that were notable in the industry.

Keep information in calendar, in a notebook, on your phone, or somewhere that you can easily refer to when necessary (during the dreaded review process), and refer to those accomplishments often. You never know when you will be in a meeting and someone will be talking about some problem that they are currently having that you have dealt with in the past. You can easily refer to those notes, and if they are reasonably detailed, you can pull out potential solutions and save the project team critical days or weeks trying to research the issue. Do not be reluctant to speak up when you have that information. We don't need to mimic our male counterparts, but looking at how they are not reluctant to suggest solutions can help us to further our careers or make a vital impact on our companies.

Don't Hide Your Sparkle

I admit that I have resorted to obfuscating my gender on occasion. I have used my first initial and last name on my job application and résumé on occasion. I have intentionally left the gender box unchecked. This is not to hide my identity; it is rather to make sure that my accomplishments and experience stand on their own. I know that anyone who really wants to know about me can use some of the information in my résumé to find me online and can identify the fact that I am a woman, but I also know that it is sometimes easier to get by the first pass at résumé analysis (and sometimes the second pass) if you are not readily identified by gender or age for that matter.

Sometimes it is better to let what you know and what you can do shine brighter than who you are. It lets you know later that what you can do speaks for you.

It's usually not as easy to hide your gender when you are talking to someone on the phone, over Skype, or in a face-to-face interview or discussion, but by that time you already have their attention and you can really show what you know.

Even more than trying to make yourself less visible, try to make yourself more visible. Don't hide in the shadows thinking that you will be noticed for the good work that you know you are doing. Know who you are and what you are good at and make sure that people get to know the real you.

I have, on more occasions than I can count, tried to hide my personality in an effort to fit into the mold that a team, a company, or a manager has thought that I should be shoe-horned into. This only manages to frustrate you and to make your job more difficult and stressful. It's hard work remembering to be someone that you're not while you are trying to do your job. Don't do it.

I have come to embrace my own personality, but it has taken many years of hiding to do that. I know that, in stressful situations, I can always find humor and make jokes that can defuse the stress. I've even managed to find a middle ground where I'm not the class clown but am a valued part of a team including my idiosyncrasies. I have worked with women who try to use brute force to accomplish their goals, and I've seen that having mixed results. If that is your personality, temper it with a bit less brashness. Some of the best women teammates I have mix brute force with humor, and it works well, particularly if you aren't afraid to sprinkle a little self-deprecating humor into relevant situations.

Find how and where you shine, and don't ever let anyone try to convince you that your way of doing things is wrong.

Communicating with Women

We have looked at how women tend to communicate (or not communicate), but there are things that people need to keep in mind when communicating with women in IT. It's not just men who need to have some gentle reminders that we are different; sometimes the worst situations are when women communicate with women.

We Aren't One of the Guys

While this should be painfully obvious, I'm afraid that the perception that we are one of the guys, or that we need to be, is getting much harder to overcome. It's even more obvious when women are in multinational and global organizations. This is in part because of the differing way that women are seen in different global cultures. It is also because in many organizations there is an official policy of inclusion and of supporting a work-life balance. However, supporting these as an organization does not mean a work-life balance is being embraced as a culture particularly in IT. The need for a work-life balance, however, is being noticed more and more by both men and women. The masculine organization where it's "all work all the time" is starting to lose more of its talent to organizations that respect a person's need to spend time with their families and still dedicate themselves to getting the work done.

We may share a lot of the same interests, but we have our own. Sometimes we feel taken aback by being told that we are the closest thing to a woman that the team has. We don't always like locker-room humor or that co-workers can swear like angry sailors. You don't have to stop being yourself or hide your own sparkle to talk to us, but keep in mind that we just might not want to engage in "mansplaining" or derogatory comments directed at ourselves or co-workers.

While I don't take it badly when the people I work with joke around (I grew up with brothers, and I'm in a male-dominated profession, so it's hard not to start to grow a thick skin) because they really do look on me as "one of the guys," it is discomforting to hear how they talk about some of the women that we are in meetings with when they walk out of the room. Objectifying women is not acceptable in any situation, and it is very unprofessional in a business setting. Yes, I have heard how boys will be boys, but it's still not acceptable, and when it gets pointed out, it causes hard feelings for days.

It is not appropriate either to use "pet names" for women or about women. I am not Honey, Sugar, or Sweetie. While this is not likely to cause most women to go running to HR, it isn't likely to have the desired effect on the conversation any more than it will if you suddenly make a big deal out of the fact that there are women present. It just makes women wonder what you would have said if we hadn't been in the room.

Even in IT, where people are usually a little more relaxed than they might be in some of the other business units, keeping things professional is a must.

Women Communicating with Women

One of the most frustrating things to deal with when you are a women is when other women talk down to you or treat you with disrespect. I don't know if the women who do this are aware that they are doing it or not. Sometimes I think that they have been in the trenches long enough that they really are starting to think along the same lines as the men who do this. They may have had to deal with this their whole careers and don't know any other way to communicate.

I think those of us who are in the situation where we are being talked down to by another women have a harder time with it than if we were being addressed by a man. It's harder to excuse away if it's a woman doing the talking, and it's much easier to internalize what is being said.

At times like this, it is good to have someone outside of the official reporting chain to talk to so you can check whether the tone or the message was overly harsh.

Key Takeaways and Lessons Learned

In this chapter, you saw that women's brains work differently from men's brains. This is not to say that either is better than the other; they are just different. Because they are different, it's important to understand that the way men and women communicate is different as well. The language centers of women's brains have markedly more neurons than men's. There has been countless studies tossed around as factual on how many more words women use in a day than men, but it's not the number of words that matter, it is how those words are processed.

Women should make effort to communicate their achievements. Publicize your accomplishments, and don't take negativity personally.

References for Further Reading

Steigler, Kay. "When Women Don't Take Credit for Their Own Good Work," *The Atlantic*. June 5, 2013, https://www.theatlantic.com/sexes/archive/2013/06/when-women-dont-take-credit-for-their-own-good-work/276555/.

Luxton, Emma. "Why Managers Give Women Less Feedback," *World Economic Forum*. Oct. 20, 2016, https://www.weforum.org/agenda/2016/10/managers-give-women-less-feedback/.

Brizendine, Louann. *The Female Brain*. Harmony, 2007.

Brizendine, Louann. *The Male Brain: A Breakthrough Understanding of How Men and Boys Think*. Harmony, 2011.

Gray, John. *Men Are from Mars, Women Are from Venus: The Classic Guide to Understanding the Opposite Sex*. Harper Paperbacks, 2012.

Gray, John. *Men Are from Mars, Women Are from Venus: Practical Guide for Improving Communication and Getting What You Want in Your Relationships*. Harper, 1993.

Gray, John. *Mars and Venus at Work: Improving Communication and Getting Results at Work*. HarperAudio, 2005.

CHAPTER 4

Electronic Communication

By far the most difficult form of communication to understand well when it comes to dealing with different cultures is electronic communication such as e-mails, text messages, online reports, instant messages, and social media. The realm of electronic communication is fraught with places where miscommunication can occur, and yet as technologists, it is where we spend the majority of our time. Taking just a few minutes to think through your message and its delivery, as well as about the impact your communication can have on the receiver or on the people who end up reading it later when they were not the originally intended audience, can have a tremendous impact on the way you are perceived. Remember, once it leaves your fingertips and is sent out into the great wide nothing of bits and bytes, it can have a life of its own.

E-mail

E-mail is thought by some to be the most marvelous tool that we have at our disposal; for others, it is the bane of our existence. Regardless of how you feel about e-mail, it is currently the way most of us communicate with the people we work with and the people we need to stay in contact with in our daily lives. I have learned the hard way that e-mail can take on a life of its own, and what you say may not be what you think you are saying.

69

© April Wells 2018
A. Wells, *The Tech Professional's Guide to Communicating in a Global Workplace*,
https://doi.org/10.1007/978-1-4842-3471-6_4

In addition, something that you think you say in confidence may end up coming back around to cause hurt feelings (or worse) once you hit Send. With e-mail, you don't have the advantage of body language or voice tone and facial expression to use as clues when communicating your message.

Make a Plan

Some e-mails don't need to be thought through extensively. You can type a quick response saying that you approve a change request, for example, but for anything more, it's better to think through the purpose of the e-mail and what exactly you want to convey.

What type of e-mail are you working on? Are you providing information? Were you responsible for something that was actionable and you are providing a response? Do you need action from someone else? Are you requesting information from someone else? Sometimes it is the case that you are continuing an ongoing dialogue.

Think through what you need to say and the tone you need to use.

I've found it to be true that everyone remembers things that are at the beginning of the e-mail or that are at the end of the mail. Things in the middle of the mail end up being less memorable to people who read. Make the first sentence or two concise and compelling. Tell them why the e-mail is important to them, why it matters that whoever is on the distribution list read the e-mail, and what action is necessary if action is required.

Subject Line

A good subject line can do half the work of the e-mail for you. It can provide people with an overview of what needs to happen or with what you need people to understand. Think of the subject line of the mail as if it were the headline of a newspaper article. If you make it compelling, the people on the distribution list will want to read the entire message.

Because you are going to be dealing with people from different cultures and from different levels of understanding of your language, it's important to use strong but simple words—words that can be translated by translation software if necessary. It's important that the words that you use are conveying exactly what you need people to know.

Take your lead from what e-mail programs do anyway. If you respond to an e-mail, the program prepends "RE:" to the subject. If you forward it, the program prepends "FW:" to the subject. By making the subject line succinct, you can make sure that even the prepending of the "FW:" or "RE:" will allow the subject to make sense.

If you are asking a question, start the subject line with the word "Question:" and then the subject of the question that you need to have addressed. Here are some examples:

> Question: What is the lead time on Linux servers for database?

> Question: Who will be testing our Oracle 12*c* upgrade?

> Question: Can we get more storage for backups?

For informational e-mails, it is a good idea to start the subject of the e-mail with "FYI:" or "Informational:" or something similar. This allows people who are just skimming their e-mail inbox that there is relevant information included but that there is nothing they are likely to need to do. This does not mean that if someone, as a consumer of the e-mail, has something relevant to add to the included information they can't include that information in a response. It is simply an indication that they don't have to feel compelled to do so.

Keep It Professional

If you're using e-mail at work, it's best to keep the e-mail professional. While this might sound obvious, it is not always a given.

Don't swear. Don't use questionable language. No name calling. Don't talk down to people. Even if you are sending an e-mail to one person only, it is simple enough for that person to forward the e-mail or include others in the response, so the manner in which you address people can quickly become common knowledge. This reflects badly on you, often with upper management who often end up on the distribution list.

Again, as with the subject line, make sure that the words you use are as concise as possible and easily translated by translation software. While it is true that most of the e-mails that we, as technologists, send are by default heavy on technology-specific words, it is also true that we can work to make our e-mails less difficult to read and translate than you may think.

Be Interested and Interesting

Sending a boring, trite, or overly complex e-mail can at best cause your particular e-mail to be skimmed and closed. At worst, it can cause your e-mails to be deleted or archived, without the ability to be accessed later if needed.

We can all probably remember the rules of interesting writing that we learned in high school or college classes. Use action verbs, mix the lengths of your sentences, and write something you would be interested in reading. If you want to find out whether your sentences contain action verbs rather than passive verbs, here's a trick: take any sentence that you're questioning and add the phrase "by zombies" to the end. If it makes perfect logical sense, try revising it.

Here's an example:

> The server will be being restarted at 8 p.m. Eastern time.

This makes perfect sense if you add "by zombies" to the end, so it's passive voice. You can easily rewrite it as follows:

> The Linux admin team will restart the server at 8
> p.m. Eastern time.

The revised version takes a few more keystrokes (and I'm all about conserving keystrokes when possible), but it is less stilted and more interesting to read the second way. What's more, if you write too many passive-voice sentences, people will tend to find the e-mails difficult to read.

Not Too Long, Not Too Short

While there are times when a single word or very short sentences are sufficient for an e-mail ("Can you run this script for me?" or "Can you reset my password?"), it is also the case when painfully short e-mails are counterproductive. E-mails that take several screen scrolls are also often not what people need or feel compelled to read.

Too short, and you will fail to provide all of the information necessary to convey your message. It leaves the reader needing to ask questions, requiring more e-mails and more thought and time to be put into the e-mails.

I've received both types of e-mails, and while I know that longer is usually much more useful than shorter, longer e-mails often take entirely too much time to pour through in order to get the most value from them. I know when I get e-mails from specific people that I need to set aside at least five minutes to read through the e-mail and an additional five or maybe ten minutes to really understand what the e-mail is trying to tell me.

If you need to write a long, in-depth, technically detailed e-mail in order to be complete in your information, writing what is akin to an e-mail novel, then by all means create that e-mail. But make sure you write it in a way that increases your chances of having the information conveyed.

If you want someone to understand what you are talking about, make your first paragraph count. Tell them what you are going to explain in the remainder of the e-mail. Then, if people have the time at this point, they can continue reading. They can make the informed decision. Once you have explained all of the things you want to convey in the e-mail, add a conclusion paragraph.

In summary, tell them what you are going to tell them (in a short, concise manner), tell them the details of what you're going to tell them, and then tell them what you told them. That way, people can consume your e-mail in the manner that best fits their requirements. You are, in fact, writing your e-mail for your reader, not for yourself.

Take Your Time

Again, while there are times when a quick e-mail or a quick response to an e-mail is the perfect solution, it is also true that you need to be able to think through exactly what you need to say in the e-mail. No one knows how long you took to write whatever comes in the e-mail. It is in your best interest to take your time and craft your e-mail well. Use spell-check and grammar check tools, make sure what you are trying to explain is clear, and make sure you are explaining it in the best way possible. It will be worth the time you spend in the long run.

When in Doubt, Get a Proofreader

Find someone where you work who you trust. It should be someone who has the grammar skills to make sure that your e-mail is what you want it to be and someone who has an understanding of the subject matter; if that's not possible, then it should at least be someone who has experience writing in the language of the e-mail.

It does not reflect badly on you if you ask for a second set of eyes or someone else's opinion. I look at it as if I'm asking someone for a code review. If I'm not certain how something is going to be taken (and often I'm accused of being to blunt) or how something is worded for accuracy, I will ask someone who's opnion I trust. It can mean the difference between having someone angry becuase you have made a cultural miss step or offended at your wording. If you are lucky enough to have someone who takes pains with word choices in your department they can make sure that you don't use then when you mean than and you don't use too when to is correct.

Do Not E-mail the Way You Talk

One lesson that I learned the hard way is that you shouldn't e-mail the way that you talk. I made the mistake of doing just that.

I was working on an issue with someone from a different department when I went home one day. I had left with what I hoped was a solution and with the understanding that things would be tested and I would get feedback on whether the solution was actually a solution. I got to work the next morning to find no word on the current status of the issue or any word from anyone on the e-mail chain.

I sent a response to the e-mail (not really knowing who all the people were on the distribution list) saying "GOOD morning! Not to beat a dead horse, but where do we stand with the issue we were working on last night?"

I got a huge lesson in e-mail etiquette that day. One of the upper managers came and called me out on the tone and wording of my e-mail. Apparently the fact that "GOOD" was in all caps (even though it is the way that I actually say "good morning") was taken as if I was angry, not just emphatic. More to the point, the distribution list on that particular e-mail chain was not only international but global in nature, and I found out that it was quite likely that someone (or more than one someone) had taken offense at my wording.

I had never met the manager I dealt with that day before. I had never actually even heard of the manager I dealt with that day. However, I was taken to task, and he explained to me all of the ways that my e-mail had been offensive or could have been offensive. The discussion was strict, and for months afterward I avoided that manager every way I could find. It was more than a year later before he and I came to an actual truce and found out that we had a lot in common; we actually became friends. We laugh about the e-mail now, but I took the whole incident very much to heart.

While I do sometimes write e-mails in a conversational manner, those are casual e-mails to family and close friends. When I compose e-mails for work, I make sure to double-check and triple-check what I write to make sure that it sounds conversational but professional.

Want to make an impression on the people you're including on your e-mail? Consider adapting your colloquial language to include some of the ways that the people you're including communicate. For example, spell words in a manner more typical of your audience than perhaps you might if it wasn't including an international audience.

Not everyone who speaks or reads English spells words in the same way. English is becoming more of a standard language in business; however, U.S. English isn't used everywhere. British English that is spoken, read, and written in many countries has different spellings for words such as color (*colour*), flavor (*flavour*), organization (*organisation*), recognize (*recognise*), and analyze (*analyse*). This shows a willingness to adapt your communication rather than expecting everyone else to adapt to yours.

In addition, sometimes you can adopt some of the ways that your audience talks to make your e-mail less stilted or less culturally one-sided. Consider changing some of your greetings or closings in different ways. Maybe say "Good day" as an opening rather than "Hi" or "Hello." It was gratifying to see the difference that incorporating "Bom Dia" (both verbally and in e-mails) into some of my discussions with people in Brazil made. Close some of your e-mails with "Cheers," "Regards," "Kind regards," or another variation. "Thanks" can sound very casual and can be interpreted as you think that the reader is doing you a service by reading your e-mail. By incorporating colloquial turns of phrase, you not only show your willingness to adapt to changes but also increase your cross-cultural vocabulary and improve your overall communication.

As one final comment on how to present your e-mail professionally in a global setting, don't assume that everyone will be reading your e-mail in the same time zone as you are writing it. Even if they are from the same company and from the same location, they might be working a different shift, on vacation, or something else that prevents them from reading "Good morning" in the morning. More to the point, however, it is a far better practice to create a time-neutral greeting that you use regardless of when you are crafting your e-mail.

Do Not Co-opt an E-mail Thread

It's important to keep the discussion on an e-mail thread relevant to the main subject of the e-mail. Don't take the e-mail and radically change the topic of discussion. If all you want is the same distribution list, copy the distribution list and start your own e-mail chain with your own subject line. You can click Reply All to the e-mail and then remove all of the information from the existing chain and change the subject line to your own subject.

For example, don't assume that by using an e-mail thread with the topic of "Friday's Pot Luck Team Lunch" that has been making the rounds of the team for several days, several times a day, that you can use that discussion but change the topic, such as asking someone to move a file from a Windows server to a Linux server that you don't have access to. You probably won't get what you need. By the time there are six or seven "RE:" headers on the subject line of the e-mail, chances are that people aren't as actively following the discussion. They are getting on with their work and believing that they can catch up with any changes in details closer to the team lunch.

This harkens back to the subject line discussion from earlier in this chapter, but in this case you need to actively change the subject of the e-mail to make it relevant or useful. In that way, you neither frustrate yourself by waiting on a request that may or may not ever come nor irritate or confuse the people still actively following the previous discussion that will read your co-opted e-mail.

Responding

The general "rules" for responding to e-mails are about the same as those for composing and sending e-mails. If you have taken the time to respond to an e-mail, in the first couple sentences reiterate what the discussion has been talking about so far. You don't have to write out everything that everyone has said so far, but putting something relevant and cogent in the first sentence or two will make it much more likely that people will quickly respond because they can quickly read it.

Sometimes it is helpful to make the subject shorter by taking out several of the "FW:" and "RE:" tags. This is not only cleaner but makes the subject easier to read when you're looking at it in a mobile e-mail client or nearly any e-mail interface. If I have to open an e-mail and scroll to see the whole subject line, I'm not apt to be as interested in the e-mail as if I can just glance at it and not have to think too much. My day is busy enough without having to deal with difficult e-mails. And it's worse when I'm only copied on it for information and I come into the chain late in the game and have to hunt for the subject to see if I even want to bother reading it now or wait until later. Figure 4-1 shows an example of what I'm talking about. I frequently am only in a place where I can look at my e-mail on my phone, and this is not a useful subject to me.

Figure 4-1. *Example of an unhelpful subject line*

Even if this e-mail were directed to me as a response, I wouldn't realize it unless I actually took the time to open it and read it, especially if whoever responded didn't put something in the first sentence to clue me in to what this was about or what it was in response to.

Think before you rush to respond to an e-mail. Think about what you would see and what you would understand by just reading the response or the subject line. While there are mail clients that you can use that will clean up your subject line for you, many still don't and you want your email to be read and as clear as possible from the beginning.

Be Careful What You Say

Don't write anything in an e-mail that you wouldn't be willing to say to someone's (anyone's) face. You never know when something like that can come back to cause you issues later. You don't know who might print it and unintentionally leave it for someone else to see; in addition, you don't know when someone will change the distribution list and include someone who would be offended by the e-mail. Worse, sometimes someone will take part of the e-mail out of context (or not so out of context) and post it somewhere or send it to someone thinking that there is no way that the quoted text could be traced back to you as the source. Sometimes it can be traced back, though, and that can lead to no end of trouble.

It's better to remember that nothing you ever write electronically (and let's face it, most of what is written today is written electronically) has any semblance of being private. It's far safer to always keep in mind that what happens digitally will outlive you and can cause you to lose a job or to have to live with hard feelings for years.

To, CC, and Blind Copy

Pay attention to where you fall on the To/CC/BCC line of any e-mail that you consider responding to. Look at that information when you read the e-mail so you can read it with the idea that you either do or don't need to take action on it.

If you are on the To line of an e-mail, that e-mail is directed at you or a group/team you are involved in. It may contain information that is particularly relevant to you. It might mean that you need to take action on whatever the content of the e-mail may be. Your response may or may not be needed, but the e-mail is of particular importance to you. If you're writing an e-mail, keep this same information in mind. Put the people on the To line that you want either to do something pertinent to the e-mail or to be particularly aware of whatever the subject matter contained in the e-mail is. If you just want someone to be aware of what is going on, the To line might not be the best place for the recipient.

CC (which stands for "carbon copy") is where a recipient should be if they are not expected to take action but rather just be aware of what is going on. I will often put my boss on the CC line of an e-mail discussing something that I'm actively working on so I know that he is aware of what is going on. While it isn't evident on a mobile e-mail client (or any other e-mail client for that matter) who is on the To or the CC line without opening the e-mail, it is still pertinent information to have when you're communicating via e-mail.

BCC is a handy when you want to have a copy of an e-mail sent to yourself without anyone knowing you're that paranoid. It's also handy for sending out information on events or sending pictures of an event to a big distribution list when you don't want someone to reply to the entire group. I will BCC my Evernote account when I want to remember a script that I've had to run that I found handy or a date that an event is going to occur that I need to remember. By putting everyone in the distribution in the BCC line, they can respond to you without everyone getting an e-mail (or 50) about how cute someone is or how excited they are for the event. In other words, putting someone on the BCC line will allow that person to respond to you without responding to everyone. I would never use BCC to keep someone in the loop on anything. If I don't want someone to know I've copied people outside a group or someone higher on the management chain than the e-mail is actually intended for, it's far better to forward the e-mail to those people with an "FYI" message rather than BCCing them. This way they will also respond to you only if they feel their response or input is necessary without accidentally replying to people who didn't know they were being informed of the discussion.

Instant Messages

If you think that people aren't reading your instant messages you send at work, you might be mistaken. Someone might not be sitting around all the time reading every word as the Enter key is pressed all over the company, but the messages are likely being stored and the data from them mined to determine whether someone is perpetuating theft or fraud. The same thing is true with your e-mails.

Many companies put the fact that they are monitoring this communication in their security handbook or the company handbook. Others aren't as open about it, but the fact that it happens is more common than you might think.

There are companies that are built on the idea that the information that is found in instant messages, chats, e-mails, and the like can be not only stored but mined for places where legal action can or should be taken.

At best there is a chance that someone could walk up and read over your shoulder. More likely it would be the case that someone might find out what was said because one of the people involved in a discussion copied a portion of the message and e-mailed it to someone because they thought that person would find it relevant.

It's also important to understand that people think of instant messages as more casual a conversation than e-mail. Communication tends to be far less formal, often lapsing into little more than technical shorthand. While it is usually the case that we share a mutual understanding of what the shorthand likely means ("thx" for thanks or thank you, "kk", or worse just "k" for okay, "wc" for you're welcome), it is still rather sloppy and unprofessional. It's also the case that instant messages are meant to be short discussions—an alternative to picking up the phone for a short call. It is not meant to convey detailed information that needs to hang around after what might occur in a "blue screen of death."

That said, however, instant messages can be a great cultural equalizer. If used with the understanding that you never know who is on the other end of the conversation and craft your message in a way that will allow anyone from any culture to easily understand your message, it can open meaningful conversation between people on different continents. Remember, it's impossible (and poor practice) to assume that because someone is in the same country, has a familiar name spelling, or works in the same company that they will automatically understand your grammar and slang. It is never good to assume anything.

Social Media

Social media (Facebook, Twitter, Instagram, and LinkedIn are just a few) has radically changed the way people interact and build their brands. While it is the case that not all social networking is accessible in every location in the world, it is also the case that in many locations it is widely accessible and used by people every day.

What you post on social media is a reflection of who you are. What you have posted can often be accessed and used by companies to determine whether they want to hire you in the future and to determine whether they want to continue your current employment. No matter what you think or what you say to yourself when you are sitting relaxing in your jammies, what you post online can come back to reflect badly on you. I know of at least one example where a Facebook post about how someone thought they were doing at a job was impetus to get that person immediately dismissed because it reflected badly on the employer.

If you want to present the best possible face to the world, create posts that can be easily translated. Most social media now has the feature of being able to be translated from the language in which it was written to another language automatically. If you make your posts simple to read and translate (not only between languages but also between generations or other intracultural divisions), it will make your posts and your information more relevant and enjoyable.

Remember, you don't know who will be reading your posts, so make them easy to read, but also write them such that they don't reflect badly on you as a person. You are building your brand with every public post you make. Make sure you are presenting the voice and the face to the world that you want to present.

Trouble Tickets

If you work in technology, it is a reality that we all, at some time, will have to put in a trouble ticket for something. Sometimes it will be with a vendor. Sometimes it will be with the internal company's help desk. Irrespective of who they are with, we will have to put them in and keep them updated.

If you have to put in a trouble ticket with a very large company (IBM, Oracle, Microsoft, and Dell are among the ones that come to mind), you will not have any idea who is going to be responding to your ticket, who will be reading it, and who will be working on the issue. It is likely that the people working on the issue will either speak the same language you do or have translation software to translate your words into their language. Again, as with e-mail, make sure that your words are clear and concise.

By keeping your updates simple to read and as timely as possible, the analyst who is working on your issue will be able to help you as quickly as possible.

The opposite is just as true. If you are on the end of a trouble ticket (or documentation referenced by a trouble ticket) in a different language, it is immensely helpful if the analyst providing you with information uses language that is easily understood and translatable. I've worked on trouble tickets where the solution or the request for information could not be copied out of the ticket and pasted into Google Translate, so I had to spend more time retyping the update than I spent providing the information necessary to process the ticket. It is immensely frustrating for someone to ask you to do something and no matter how you try to translate it you have to go to someone who is a native speaker to find out what is being asked of you.

Documentation

Documentation is typically electronic these days. It may reside on an internal wiki site, or it may reside on a shared drive or SharePoint, but rarely is any documentation in hard copy form unless someone prints it for the purpose of marking it up.

There are many best practices for writing this documentation. Companies tend to standardize on the way they want the documentation written, formatted, and saved. It is also the case that documentation frequently doesn't conform to these standards. It's important to spell out the full commands necessary to accomplish whatever is being described by the documentation in a way that anyone using it can accomplish the desired outcomes. Simply telling someone what command should be used is often not sufficient and not translatable into other languages.

Again, simple and concise language without a lot of extra information is better when you need to have it translated. Text documents, PDFs, and office suite documents are easily ported into a translation program with a result in readable format if you're lucky. I've had the misfortune of trying to translate different installation and administration documents for a software product I was responsible for implementing. No matter how I tried converting the language it was written in to one I could read, I always came up with unintelligible garbage. It can be incredibly frustrating.

If you are writing documentation, make sure you run it through a translation program on an independent computer to determine whether it will translate to several of the more common languages without returning page after page of unprintable and unreadable characters. Make your documentation simple to use and as useful as possible.

Text Messages

My smartphone is my chosen form of communication. By carrying my work smartphone with me everywhere I go, I am able to stay in communication with people I work with and with people who need to contact me who chose to not do so via voice communication. As with instant messages, it is important to make these communication avenues as useful and simple to read as possible. Because we work in organizations that span generations as well as, oftentimes, language differences, relying on text speak or text shortcuts can lead to misunderstandings and misimpressions from the intended audience.

In fact, apps are available that will translate one language of text message to another, which will allow you to span the language barrier, but this is not the only barrier to communication clarity that we face.

I am one of the lucky "older Americans" who doesn't have trouble making the leap in communication technology. I am as comfortable using my smartphone as I am using a computer. The difficulty arises when I need to use my phone to read long e-mails or verbose text messages. I have actually taken jibes about the fact that I prefer using what is now often termed a *phablet* because it has a larger display screen than a regular smartphone.

So, keep in mind that cross-cultural communication challenges are not only those that span languages but also those that span generations.

Key Takeaways and Lessons Learned

We live in a continuously connected world. Electronic communication is everywhere, and we all have to deal with it at work via e-mail, instant messaging, electronic reports, or our dreaded performance appraisals. Putting some thought into what you write and making sure that your message is written in a way that will make sure it is acted upon in a timely manner can keep everyone from being unduly stressed and can advance projects more quickly.

Remember, what you write electronically can take on a life of its own. Make sure what you have written reflects what you want people to remember about you.

References for Further Reading

Bernoff, Josh. *Writing Without Bullshit: Boost Your Career by Saying What You Mean.* HarperBusiness, 2016.

Rubin, Danny. *Wait, How Do I Write This Email? Game-Changing Templates for Networking and the Job Search.* News to Live By, 2015.

Osman, Hassan. *Don't Reply All: 18 Email Tactics That Help You Write Better Emails and Improve Communication with Your Team.* Amazon Kindle edition, 2015.\

CHAPTER 5

Slang, Jargon, and More

Slang consists of words used only by specific social groups, such as teenagers or soldiers.

Idioms are a group of words that seem to have a meaning that you can't deduce easily from those around them. The words in an idiom have meanings on their own, but together they have a completely different meaning.

A *colloquialism* is any word or phrase that is not formal, in other words, one that is usually used in casual conversation.

People in IT tend to have their own sublanguage that, for the most part, the people we work with understand. When a group of people has a subset of language that only they understand, the words are called *jargon*. People in IT tend to understand IT words. While some of us who have been in the trenches longer have a broader set of words that sometimes our newer team members might not always understand, the jargon that we use is unique to us.

This is not the case with everyone we work with, however.

Few of us work in a vacuum. We spend time in meetings interacting with people who are from different departments (that have different sets of jargon and slang), and sometimes this leads to misunderstandings or miscommunication.

© April Wells 2018
A. Wells, *The Tech Professional's Guide to Communicating in a Global Workplace*,
https://doi.org/10.1007/978-1-4842-3471-6_5

Worse, sometimes we inadvertently leave people with hard feelings because of the things we have said. It is much harder to mend professional relationships than it is to think through what you are saying (or not saying) and not have the hard feelings happen to begin with.

In this chapter, we will look at some common ways that we can make missteps when communicating and how we can avoid this in the future.

Slang

Slang is highly informal language in either written or spoken communication. It includes words and phrases that are typically understood primarily either in a particular context, during a particular point in history, or by a certain group of people. As technology processionals, slang has a tendency to sneak into our communication. There are even situations where that is not only acceptable but to some degree expected. However, slang is not easily understood by people not within the group or who don't understand the context.

To a great extent, slang is often considered to be primarily used by the younger people in a culture and used by the uneducated or undereducated in a society.

Slang doesn't always translate well between different cultures in different countries, and oftentimes it doesn't translate well between different cultures within the same country or different translations of the same language. For example, Colombian Spanish has different slang translations than Argentine Spanish, and Spanish (while having the same roots) has completely different slang meanings and translations than Portuguese.

Within one part of the United States even, it's easy for those of us who know teenagers and young adults to think of examples. I've heard things like "Did you see Janet's new sweater? It's totally wicked." Taken literally, that would mean the sweater was evil or bad. With young adults, however, it means that Janet's sweater is really nice, pretty, or something that would be nice to have.

Listening to this slang when you are from the same place (overhearing two teenagers talking when you are from the same city or state) but without the frame of reference that "wicked" means good or awesome, you could come away with very different ideas about Janet's sweater.

Now imagine being from another country or culture and trying to understand this conversation. You might even have to translate this conversation into another language for a friend to understand it. The friend will probably come away with a very different idea of what is being said than the intention.

In addition, slang doesn't tend to stand the test of time. While there are times that slang from a given point in time makes it into normal, everyday vernacular (even into Webster's and the Oxford dictionaries), it is far more common that it doesn't.

For example, a *square* in the 1950s in the United States would have been understood to be someone boring or unpopular. Referring to someone that way in 2017 might get you a confused look or get you ridiculed. It is the case, however, that people who were young adults at a given point of time (the 1950s, for example) might retain the slang in their day-to-day communication.

Context is everything with slang, and that's another reason to avoid it when you can. *Hot*, in connection to a human, probably means very attractive. *Hot* in connection to a ring or a watch is much more likely to mean it's been stolen. I've actually heard someone in a server room make this statement: "Did you see the (server) cluster over there? It's hot." In a sentence like that, it could take on any of three meanings. It might be running at a temperature higher than normal, it might be an incredibly impressive cluster, or it may actually have been stolen. Sometimes it is better to be thought to be boring rather than to be completely misunderstood.

Idioms/Metaphors

The use of idioms is universal, and idioms are endemic to each given culture or locality. They make some sense to the people in a given culture, but they often don't make sense to people outside of that culture. Worse, they can cause startling reactions from people outside of that culture.

Idioms take words that are common and make changes in the way that those words are combined to make sense to the culture that is using them, but the combination of words might not make sense to others or if you take the words literally.

You might think that is an exaggeration. However, let me illustrate. Several years ago, Sara was working on an issue on a database. She asked her co-workers if anyone had any concerns with her dropping a table that appeared to be a temporary table. One of the other people in the room told her that Scott is usually the one that deals with that database, and everyone knows that Scott is anal about his databases. José (who has been in the country for just a handful of years from Mexico City at the time) looked up from his computer with shock in his eyes. It took ten minutes for the people in the room to explain to José what they meant by the idiom (Scott is anal retentive when it comes to the database, meaning has a desire to be overly orderly). When Scott came back after his vacation, the discussion of what was going on with the database became the topic of conversation. His comment, without ever hearing the discussion about the idiom, was this: "Oh, yeah, everyone knows how anal I am about that database." The story of the conversation became an artifact in that company.

It's also an interesting case in point as to what can happen when you use casual language that might not translate well between cultures even if the people all speak the same language.

When I was starting to look at what pitfalls can happen with communication and cultures, idioms became really interesting to me.

The United States is ripe with them. But other countries have just as many and just as confusing ones (Table 5-1).

Table 5-1. *Examples of Idioms*

Country	Idiom	Meaning
United States	Like putting lipstick on a pig.	To make something appear better without actually improving anything about it.
	It's a piece a cake.	Something is very easy.
	Adding fuel to the fire.	Making matters worse.
	Pushing the envelope.	Stretching the boundaries.
	Being anal about something.	To be obsessive or pay great attention to something.
Germany	You have tomatoes on your eyes.	You're not seeing what is obvious to others.
	I only understand the train station.	I don't have any idea what they are talking about.
Swedish	There's no cow on the ice.	There's no need to worry.
	Slide in on a shrimp sandwich.	Someone who didn't need to be working.
Thailand	Take ears to the field, take eyes to the farm.	Don't pay any attention.
	The hen sees the snake's feet, and the snake sees the hen's boobs.	Two people have known all of each other's secrets.

(continued)

Table 5-1. (*continued*)

Country	Idiom	Meaning
Latvian	To blow little ducks.	To talk nonsense, to lie.
French	To swallow grass snakes.	Being so insulted that you can't speak.
	Jump from the cock to the donkey.	To keep changing topics without logic.
	They looked at each other like ceramic dogs.	Look at each other disgustedly.
Russian	Galloping across Europe.	To do something haphazardly.
	Thief has a burning hat.	An uneasy conscience that betrays itself.
	You can sharpen with an ax on top of his head.	He is hard-headed, stubborn.
Portuguese	He who doesn't have a dog hunts with a cat.	Make the most of what you have.
	Push it with your belly.	Keep postponing something important.
	Pay the duck.	Take the blame for something you didn't do.
Polish	Elephant stomped on your ear.	You're tone deaf.
	He just fell from a Christmas tree.	You're not very well informed.
Japanese	Wear a cat on one's head.	Pretending to be a nice person.
	To borrow a cat's paws.	So busy that you would even be willing to accept help from a cat's paws.
	Cat's forehead.	A tiny space.
	Cat tongue.	Wait until hot food cools to eat it.

Colloquialisms

Colloquialisms are those unique parts of speech that show up when you are talking, usually casually, to people who you interact with on a daily basis. They are often regional in nature and tend to be some of the words and phrases that can mark someone as having come from a particular location.

For example, I grew up in Western Pennsylvania and while some people can pick up on that fact by what remains of the accent that I doubtless still have to one degree or another, it is more often the words or pronunciation of words that can give it away. The first word that I can remember trying to cleanse from my vocabulary was *mirrow* (you know, the shiny glass thing you look in to comb your hair or shave or brush your teeth). I grew up pronouncing it "mirrow." It was pointed out to me how incorrect that was—that it is "mirror." I worked at saying it how it was supposed to be said to clean up one little corner of my vocabulary.

Over the years, I've realized other things, such as *yinz* isn't a word. It is commonly used by people in the Pittsburgh area to mean "you" (usually the plural "you" of talking to a group). In addition, *ain't* has been a source of contention for decades at least.

It is a fact, however, that sometimes colloquialisms end up being a somewhat sanctioned part of speech by virtue of making it into the dictionary.

It is advantageous to recognize when idioms are cropping up in conversation (you can usually tell by the puzzled looks that people give you) and work to remove them from your business conversations. It takes a little more time, but it pays off in the end when everyone better understands what you are saying.

Emojis, Acronyms, and Text Shortcuts

Keep in mind that you're communicating in a professional environment, and even when you're not, if you're communicating publicly, you are still communicating in a professional environment. When you're typing, many software programs will automatically translate code snippets that include semicolons or colons and parentheses into emoji smiley faces, remember that you are in a professional environment and double checking what you are sending before it is sent will leave the reader with a complete understanding of what you are really saying.

Emojis, those cute little pictures that exist in various electronic genres, are often used to give text "color." Emojis are the digital equivalent to body language; they include facial expression pictures, common objects, people, places, weather, and animals. While they often easily translate between cultures, they don't have a place in professional communication.

In general, don't take shortcuts in your communication. It takes just a few more keystrokes to type out "okay" or "OK" rather than just a simple "k." "Thank you" and "you're welcome" and "no problem" are often shortened to *tx*, *wc*, and *np* when texting or writing in instant messengers, but they creep in to other written communication as well. We might, for the most part, understand what is meant, but it leaves us with a less than professional appearance.

Humor

It was pointed out to me by a wise man that you need to be cautious using humor when you're writing something that someone globally will be reading. This is particularly true of sarcasm and dry humor. You should never lose your sense of humor, but you should be cautious about how you use it. Different cultures take a different view of humor and find different things to be humorous.

The United States, you will find, has a general overall acceptance and even an expectation of humor. Laughter, and by extension humor, is generally helpful for easing stressful situations and can release nervous energy that might otherwise turn into something less productive. It can provide an outlet for fear or anger if channeled constructively.

While it is true that humor is universal, it is also true that there is no universally humorous joke. What is hilariously funny to one person may be questionable or offensive to another person within the same culture; therefore, it is even more difficult to find humor that translates across cultures. There are some nearly universal truths, however. People of all cultures tend to laugh at incongruities, extreme exaggeration, understatement or overstatement, and irony.

While the degree to which anything is funny is dependent largely on the audience and the situation, it is interesting to note that there are similarities.

Stupid Dog

I have successfully lightened the mood in tense situations by using humor. One way is to interject humor into a situation by diverting attention (and usually blame for whatever the situation is) to "the dog." At my house, no matter what happens, it is the fault of the "stupid dog." Whether the peanut butter was left open on the counter, the front door was left open, laundry was left all over the bathroom floor, or what have you, I say something like "Stupid dog. I hate when she does that." It usually gets the point across that something isn't exactly right, without actually pointing fingers or assigning blame. It usually makes people relax and smile when they realize that the situation isn't nearly as horrible as it could be.

Humor can also be offensive to different cultures or in certain situations. Be mindful of who your audience is and whether the situation warrants the risk. Worse, depending on the joke and the audience, it can land you in trouble with HR if the jokes are offensive or off-color.

Laughing at Our Own Mistakes

One of the best uses of humor, particularly when dealing with differences in cultures, is when we can find situations to laugh at ourselves and our own mistakes. This is particularly effective when we make mistakes in language usage, cultural mistakes, or unintentional blunders.

It is not, however, acceptable to laugh at someone else's mistakes unless they are the ones who start by finding the humor in the situation. While there are times when the slip is almost impossible to not notice, it is better to gently point out the mistake (if the person doesn't know that they made it) privately. Explain the mistake and offer advice on how better to have phrased something. One example of this happened in my Spanish class when I was in college. It was, at the time, pointed out with humor that one should never use *anos* (the plural of "anus") when one means *años* (the plural of "year") with someone who is Spanish speaking. The words are easy enough to mispronounce, but the meaning conveyed can be vastly different and in this case offensive. It can make the difference between wishing someone "feliz cumpleaños" (Happy Birthday) and wishing them Happy Birth Butt.

There are other somewhat startling Spanish mistakes people have made when trying to communicate with only a bit of understanding. For example, someone who is vegetarian, or vegan, might want to impart that information to a co-worker. "Yo como vegetales" would be the way you would want to give them that information. "Yo como vegetarianos," however, might make your audience aghast as you have just told them that you eat vegetarians.

Take the time to do your research. It can make all the difference.

Rough Language

While it can be argued that political correctness sometimes goes a bit overboard, you should always second-guess yourself when thinking about whether a word or phrase might be found offensive to someone. Yes, there are times when reading and rereading for political correctness leaves communication dry, uninteresting, and with a narrow vocabulary and stilted phrasing, but there are always extremes and in the extremes is not where you want to be.

Situations can become tense in work environments, and you need to take a deep breath and make sure that you are not leaving everyone around you feeling like a powder keg is getting ready to explode. Anger is easy to detect, and anger or frustration can lead to saying things that you will likely regret later.

Even the mellowest employee can get so frustrated that they cut loose with an expletive or a show of temper. I will never forget the day when one of my co-workers who rarely exhibits any negative emotion whatsoever slammed his notebook down on his desk, roughly undocked his laptop from its docking station, and shoved it into his backpack and walked out of work in the middle of the day simply saying "I'm so done with this whole stupid mess!" For him, it was the equivalent of the animated character Donald Duck throwing a temper tantrum.

Other people find the use of explosives to be their common vocabulary. We have all dealt with them. These are the people who cannot finish a conversation without at least one expletive, typically far more than one. Sometimes they are easy to ignore. Sometimes they make everyone uncomfortable yet seem totally oblivious of the fact.

It seems simple enough to say that you should act in a professional manner and keep rough language out of your vocabulary, but in certain situations it is difficult to know what that rough language is in a given situation or within a given culture.

An example? In the United States, the sentence "The bloody neighbor was in the driveway" means that the person in the driveway was bleeding or had been splashed with blood.

The same sentence, in the United Kingdom, implies anything from a strong intensifier referring to the neighbor to a profane expletive referring to the neighbor. Granted, the sentence would not likely be uttered in a business setting, but it stands as a good example.

Did you tell the girl at the reception desk at the hotel in England that you "love her bangs"? You probably would be telling her that you really like what the hair stylist (or maybe she herself) did with the part of her hair that covers her forehead. In British English, those are referred to as her *fringe*. Telling her that you love her bangs is akin to telling her that you love having sex with her. It might elicit humor, or it could get you punched if her partner were around.

Don't think that it happens only on one side of the Atlantic.

A woman traveler checking in to a hotel might want to be woken up at 6 am. She might tell the desk clerk to "knock her up at 6 a.m." She believes she is asking for a wake-up call. What might be interpreted in the United States is that she wants to be impregnated at 6 a.m.

Think this kind of misunderstanding can't happen with people you are interacting with in a business setting? I learned differently.

I was on an implementation team in Brazil. When the project was just getting underway, people on the team were learning about each other in casual conversation amongst themselves. One of the topics of conversation was where you live. The topic wandered around to the kind of houses people live in. I made the statement that "I don't know. I guess I just live in an ordinary house in an ordinary neighborhood." Again, this statement in the United States would imply that my house, and my neighborhood, is pretty much a typical house. It's not anything special, and it's not a house on either end of the mansion to homeless spectrum. In Brazil or Argentina, saying that someone else's house is ordinary would be implying that they are less able to provide for their family, and syaing your own house is ordinary would imply you are self depricating. The difference between a typical house and an ordinary house are subtle but the implication to the audience can be much stronger.

In Brazil (and as I came to learn later, in other Latin American or Central/South American countries as well), referring to something (or someone) as *ordinary* is a rather strong slight. It implies that what or who you are talking about is less desirable; it's an insult.

No one would likely deliberately use language that would offend others, particularly in a business setting, but it is important to remember that no matter what language you use, you have to think about this because you can never tell who might find what you are saying off-putting or offensive.

While passion in your job is commendable, it is best to just curb your instincts to vent in the moment, walk away, and find your own place to vent privately. I learned a long time ago that it is therapeutic to walk outside and scream into the wind. If it is windy, it can cover your voice. If it is not, people tend to just give you really weird looks and avoid you (which is never a bad thing when you are in this kind of mood). The walk will help diffuse your own emotions, and the people who would think badly of you will be far enough away that they will not be witness to the outburst.

Jargon and Acronyms

Jargon refers to those special words, abbreviations, or expressions that are used specifically by one profession, group, or culture that are not as easily understood by people outside of that group.

For the most part, we work either with technology or in IT. This means that we tend to have our own subset of language that we use regularly. We have our own jargon. This is not to say that this is right or wrong in any way. Sit in a meeting with people from accounting, finance, or HR and you learn that people in IT aren't the only ones who have their own set of words that they use that might not be easily understood by people in other parts of business or that might be outright misunderstood by them.

Oftentimes the words we use, or the words that others use when we are in meetings with them, can lead to detrimental misunderstandings. Think I might be overstating the problem? Probably the best way to understand what I'm talking about is to look at some examples.

Those of us who use Unix or Linux might understand the word sticky to imply that the 'bit' of the file permissions that are set on a file or a directory that allow only the owner of the file. (or root) to delete or rename the file. In web design or in marketing, something being sticky might refer to the ability to retian an end user of the interface or product that is being referenced. A website that is successfully sticky encourages users to stay longer than they might otherwise have stayed or to return again and again. To the parent of a happy toddler, sticky would likely refer to the fingers of their progeny. Sticky can be used by different parts of the business, or different elements in everyday life, to mean vastly different things and without the understanding of what is meant, misunderstadnings ensue.

If you are in the United States, you might use the terms *hotel* and *motel* interchangeably. You might refer to a hotel as a place where the door that you to enter the room is inside the building and accessed from an internal hallway, and a motel is a place where the room is accessed from outside of the building from external walkways. Both of these places are, typically, rented by the night and are used by individuals, families, personal, or business situations. In Brazil you go to a hotel if you are looking for a reputable place to stay the night. You go to a motel if you are looking for a place for a sexual encounter. Referring to the wrong one in polite conversation will likely get you some misunderstanding looks.

As another example, what do you think of if I simply say "PA"? While this is an abbreviation, it is also situational jargon. I grew up in Western Pennsylvania. It is the case that I usually think first about the state I grew up in when I hear or read something referring to PA. But what does PA mean to you? If you are at your doctor's office, it might be the physician's assistant who sees you either before or instead of the actual doctor. In a school, you might hear an announcement coming over the PA (the public address system). Within a meeting or in a discussion at work, I might hear "Our PA will have to deal with that request," and for my organization that could either mean personal assistant (secretary), professional assistant (what other places often call interns), or purchasing agent. If you work in Hollywood, you would be referring to the production assistant on set. The setting, in this case, would likely dictate which of these people would be responsible for whatever request you are talking about. But without external context, there is a likelihood that there would be misunderstanding (Table 5-2).

Table 5-2. *Examples of Acronyms and Their Different Meanings*

	Business	**IT**	**Common**
BCP	Bureau or consumer protection	Business continuity planning	
ATM	Automatic teller machine	Asynchronous transfer mode	At the moment
AP	Accounts payable	Access point	Attitude problem
RCA	Revealed comparative advantage (economics)	Root-cause analysis	Radio Corporation of America
CPA	Certified public accountant	Cost per action	Car park assistant
DR	Discount rate	Disaster recovery	Drive
ROI	Return on investment	Read-only information	Rules of interaction
POS	Public offering statement	Point of sale	Piece of... stuff (polite form)

Imagine how difficult it can get when technologists are talking to business people without defining the terms that you are using in a given conversation. It can be difficlut and frustrating for people on all sides of the conversation.

Acronyms can be easily misunderstood even within a given culture or group. If we look at a family as its own group or culture, even acronyms used by members of that group can be seriously misunderstood. My daughter came home one day and told me that she was thinking about going into CIA at least for a few years. Needless to say, I was not thrilled at the thought of my youngest considering going into the Central Intelligence Agency! She looked at me like I was an idiot because she wanted (still wants to, to be honest) to go to the Cleveland Institute of Art.

CIA could mean any of the following:

Certified internal auditor

Central Intelligence Agency

Cleveland Institute of Art

Culinary Institute of America

Cash in advance

Computer interface adapter

Confidentially, integrity, and availability

These are just a few of the meanings that are common in the United States. Add in other countries and other cultures, and there can be almost endless misunderstandings. If you are using what you believe to be jargon, it is always best to, at the very least, define the terms you are using at least once in a meeting or spell them out in an e-mail the first time you use them. This makes sure everyone knows the meaning of the words you are using, and it removes as much confusion as possible.

Key Takeaways and Lessons Learned

Everyone uses humor, slang, idioms, and acronyms in their everyday interactions. They are part of who we are and how we define ourselves. The important thing, however, is to remember that you can't always be sure that the person hearing you, or reading your words, is going to understand what you mean. This is particularly true when dealing with people from other parts of the company or other parts of the world. It's always best to do a little research up front on who your audience is and make sure that the message you are conveying is the message that you mean to convey.

Also, workplaces can be stressful or tense. Resorting to rough language, swearing, and angry outbursts is not acceptable in a business situation. If you are witness to an angry, inappropriate outburst, it may be time to suggest that everyone take a break or to later point out where the person could have behaved more appropriately if you are in a position to make such a suggestion.

References for Further Reading

"What is the difference between abbreviations and acronyms?" English Language Smart Words. www.smart-words.org/abbreviations/text.html.

"Acronyms and Abbreviations." Emoticons & Smiley Page. www.muller-godschalk.com/acronyms.html.

"Common Acronyms." Your Dictionary. http://abbreviations.yourdictionary.com/articles/common-accronyms.html.

"40 brilliant idioms that simply can't be translated literally." TED Blog. https://blog.ted.com/40-idioms-that-cant-be-translated-literally/.

"Don't Let Go of the Potato: A Foreign Idiom Quiz." The Atlantic. https://www.theatlantic.com/international/archive/2014/12/guess-that-foreign-idiom/383654/.

"Idioms and sayings in various languages." Omniglot. https://omniglot.com/language/idioms/index.php.

"The best idioms from around the world, ranked." Quartz. https://qz.com/402739/the-best-idioms-from-around-the-world-ranked/.

CHAPTER 6

Telephone and Face-to-Face Communication

As Peter Drucker said, "The most important thing in communication is hearing what isn't said."

While this might sound odd, it is very true and most applicable when communicating human to human without your computer getting in the way. When you can hear someone's voice and they can hear yours, it is much simpler to hear not only what is being said but also what is *not* being said. When you can hear the tone of voice, you can hear implied sarcasm. You can hear a gentle friendly tone or a cold tense one. This doesn't always come through in electronic communication.

As hard as it for many technologists to really thrive in human-to-human communication, either through a phone or without any sort of technology intervention, it is a necessary evil. When communicating one to one, working in groups, and presenting in front of an audience, we have to come out from behind our keyboards and work in the real world. At these times, we need to take special considerations into account when we are communicating with people without technology intervention.

107

© April Wells 2018
A. Wells, *The Tech Professional's Guide to Communicating in a Global Workplace*,
https://doi.org/10.1007/978-1-4842-3471-6_6

Phone

We have all had phone calls with people who sound pleasant and who make the phone call as enjoyable as it can be. We have also had those phone calls that seem to drag on forever and that leave us feeling like the person on the other end just doesn't "get" phone calls. While it is true that the telephone does allow for technology to intervene between people, it is also the case that there are specific things we need to remember when communicating in this way. One of the best things, technologically speaking, to happen to telephone conversations was the advent of caller ID. The caller ID feature means people know who is calling and can avoid calls they don't want to take; in addition, it allows you to get yourself ready for the call and the caller because it shows who is calling before you answer the call. Caller ID may only give you the name of a company on the other end, but it is a boon to communication.

You look at your phone, see who is calling, and smile. Or you look at your phone, see who is calling, and cringe. Both are valid responses to caller ID.

Even when you don't know who is on the other end of the line, caller ID may help you recognize that you need to change your greeting or your mannerisms in given situations. Whether it is your boss, your co-worker, your subordinate, or someone you don't even know calling, you probably have a script in your head on how to deal with phone calls.

In general, the following tips are good telephone etiquette:

- Answer the phone as promptly as possible. Custom dictates that you try to answer by the third ring. This is probably because many answering machines are designed to pick up after the third ring.

- Keep a smile in your voice (even if you might not mean it). It doesn't matter if you want to talk to the person calling or not. If there is caller ID, call the person on the other end by name. If it is a company name that shows up on your caller ID, you may not be able to call them by name, but you can answer with a smile in your voice. Even if you don't mean it, it sounds as if you do. And it sounds as if the caller has your undivided attention.

- Make sure you mention your company name as well as your name if you are answering your work phone. The security part of my brain has a problem with this, mostly because sometimes people aren't aware that they are getting lucky and getting a company when they are out phishing. But in general, it is better to err on the side of making sure that whoever is calling knows not only who they are talking to (your name) but also what company they have been connected to (in case it is a wrong number or so they are aware of who it is that you represent).

- Speak clearly. While this is a good rule in general, it is particularly important when you are communicating with people who speak or listen differently from you. Even more important, you will likely not realize when someone is listening differently from you. While we often realize that people from other countries who speak English (or whatever language is not your primary language) as a second language might need us to slow down or annunciate more clearly, we don't, however, think that people who speak the same language that we do would require the same careful speaking. It may be the case that the person on the other end of your phone conversation is using a captioned telephone for the hearing impaired. Or the person might be from a different part of the country. I've been told that people from the northeast of the

109

United States speak more quickly than people from the southern states. Also, people who are differently abled might communicate differently.

- Respond to voice mails promptly. There are many cultures (and many people in general) that view timely responses to be more professional. Time, in general, for many cultures is critical for relationships and therefore business relationships. Promptness (for meetings, for responses to e-mail or voice mail, etc.) is vital. It is important that you plan for the differences in time use when scheduling and attending meetings and conference calls, planning projects, or anticipating travel.

- Ask permission before putting someone on hold. There is a corollary to this. I have the worst time transferring calls when someone gets me in error and asks to be put in touch with the right person. Just because I work in IT doesn't mean I have the wherewithal to really understand the phone system. Apologize in advance for disconnecting someone and provide the caller with the correct phone number or extension before you try to transfer the call (unless of course it is a phishing call). I know I am not the only one who has this issue because I've lost count of the number of times I have been inadvertently (I hope) hung up on in an attempt to transfer my call.

- Avoid sneezing or coughing into the phone. I know from personal experience that while I'm on the phone to someone and they do sneeze or cough (or use a can opener or eat or chew gum or run water or use the bathroom), it is amplified extensively because I use a headset when I am on the phone. What might sound perfectly normal when I'm on a handset is nearly painful when I'm using a headset. And, honestly, who wants to listen to what you are doing in the background?

- Don't interrupt the caller. Interrupting callers, or any other speaker, is poor manners and considered not professional in most corporate cultures. Remember, cultural is not only a matter of where you are from in the world but also where you are in the realm of the company.

- Don't use phrases like "That's not my job" or "That's not my responsibility" or "That's not my department." Those kinds of phrases don't sound professional; they leave the caller feeling like they are at fault for getting the wrong department (often, for getting the wrong department *again*) or like they are an irritant. If you have to point the caller to another department, make sure they are not left feeling like it is their fault or that they are an inconvenience.

- Use speaker phone judiciously when you are speaking person to person and make sure that the person on the other end of the line is OK with that. When I am working on an issue with my computer or other technology and I initiate a call with the help desk, I use speaker phone so I can use both hands on the computer, router, television, or what have you; however, it is more courteous to use a headset if that is an option than to use speaker phone.

Corporate cultures, socioeconomic cultures, and global cultures all have their own view of telephone etiquette, but in general, the previous tips are best practices that should keep you in good standing in your professional and personal life.

Face to Face

Telephone communication, to some extent, still has technology as an intermediary. Face-to-face communication has its own idiosyncrasies. When you can see the person you're talking to, when you can observe their expressions and body language, it adds entirely new dimensions to the conversation.

Meetings

If you are planning or running a meeting for people across a spectrum of cultures, you should be aware of the different approaches of different cultures. Even different levels of an organization have their own ideas on what it means to attend a meeting and who should be in charge. Crossing global cultures in meetings adds considerations of whose ideas and preferences should be the default in the given situation and who is likely to not be heard.

Above all, as in any communication situation, it's important to approach all situations with an open mind and a good sense of humor. You likely already have a pretty decent grasp of the obvious ins and outs of meetings, so it's really just a matter of refining what you already know.

Where to Sit

One of the biggest things to understand in cross-cultural meetings is where people sit (or are supposed to sit) in the meeting. The rules of where the people sit are rather fluid within an organization, or within a department within an organization.

The person who sits at the head of the table traditionally is the boss. So, unless the manager is the first to enter the meeting and sits somewhere else, it is usually good to leave the head of the conference room table available for the most senior manager to use should she choose. If there is no manager or no "boss" in the meeting, this seat is usually taken by the person leading the meeting. It is the seat of power. If the meeting is in any way contentious, the people who sit to the right and left of the head of the table are the supporting managers or leaders who support the position of the person who is sitting at the head of the table.

The seat at the foot of the table, opposite the head of the table, is usually allowed to be used by the most senior manager who has a different agenda from the manager running the meeting. If there is not contention in the meeting agenda, the seat at the foot of the table is usually taken by the second most senior meeting attendee. To his right and left are the people who are most likely to support his position. An obvious exception to this loose rule is in meeting rooms where there is a screen at the head or foot (or both) of a meeting room. If there is projection hardware included in the room, it is typically given a "seat" of honor in the room as it will likely be the focus of nearly everyone's attention.

These rules are usually only followed during very formal meetings or negotiations. They are far less likely to be followed in companies where meeting rooms are at a premium, in which case the seats are usually taken in a first-come first-serve basis. In all cases, and in the case of meetings where rooms are at a premium and seats are even more so, it is important to arrive at meetings promptly. If you are late to the meeting, you stand a better than average chance of offending the meeting organizer, and if you are late enough to a meeting room with limited seating, you may find yourself sitting against the wall or standing, making you more likely to not be noticed if you want to interject comments in the meeting.

Seats along the edges of a meeting room table are typically less favorable to attendees because it is sometimes difficult to see all of the other attendees, and you may not be able to see the effect of the speakers who are also sitting along the sides of the table.

In general, it is best to arrive early to a meeting so you can get a seat, especially one where you feel most comfortable and that is applicable to your position in the meeting's topic.

It is also best for people who aren't going to take active part in the discussion to sit against the wall and leave table seats for people who are taking active parts.

If you know in advance that you are going to have to make an early exit from the meeting, all efforts should be made to sit as near to the door as possible. This makes your anticipated exit as unobtrusive as possible.

Say What

Another meeting question is whether off-topic or pre-meeting chitchat is permitted. I have been in meetings where the topic of the discussion is only a general suggestion and where the discussion is actually more of a free-for-all. I have also been, ironically, in a brainstorming meeting where the meeting organizer insisted that the meeting have a strict agenda and that only the speakers on the agenda actually say anything; this was the single weirdest brainstorming meeting ever. No free thinking was allowed; we were only going to discuss what we already decided were the key points, and we could not speak unless our ideas had already been prearranged with the meeting organizer.

Countries like Brazil tend to be less formal when it comes to meetings. Because they generally value relationships as much as anything in business situations, there is often no formal agenda, and pre-meeting discussion is common, as are side conversation interruptions during the meeting. Further, in Brazil, the conversation is typically direct, and you don't have to read anything into discussions.

Germany and UK meetings, conversely, might have discussions before the meeting but typically have an agenda that should be adhered to for the discussion. Few interruptions are tolerated, and the discussion is very direct, almost painfully direct in the manner of discussion.

Japan and China meetings likely have an agenda to stick to, and interruptions are frowned upon. Pre-meeting discussions are welcome and are often used as a means to enhance business relationships. Conversation style, conversely, is indirect, with the intention of saving face and protecting the honor of all meeting attendees. Therefore, no one will likely directly say "no" to something but would likely rather say "possibly."

The United States and Canada have commonalities in that there are likely no strict agendas to be followed, and interrupting the topic discussion is frowned upon. Canadians likely would not engage in pre-meeting discussions and are more likely to be indirect.

While naturally these are generalities and you should never make blanket statements about any culture, they are things to be taken into account when scheduling meetings, determining how much time to allow for the meeting, and making sure that no one becomes offended.

Time in Meetings

In international and global organizations, it's important to understand the differences in the way that people view meetings. Because conference calls and video conference calls are more common today than ever before, you need to be aware of time offsets and understand when your conference call is likely to be outside of office hours.

Courtesy and logic would dictate that if you actually want someone in the United States to attend your 6 a.m. Eastern time meeting and you are in Italy (for example), don't send the invitation at 9 a.m. local Italy time the same day and then be surprised that the New York invitees weren't awake to get the invitations. If you are depending on information provided by the people who were not awake to get your invitation, your meeting is likely to be fruitless.

Not only is time relevant when crossing time zones, but many cultures are more time oriented than others. British and German organizations, for example, pay close attention to time boundaries (the beginning and ending of meetings). If you are meeting with someone in or from Brazil or Chile, for example, you might find that meeting times are more of a general parameter and that starting and ending times may actually vary from the "scheduled" time by a margin. It is disconcerting for both parties if someone from Brazil is hosting a meeting with someone from Germany and the host is running five or so minutes late for the meeting. The Brazilian might not understand the frustration that the German feels with the lateness in starting, and the German is likely to be frustrated at what he views as wasting time that was set aside for the meeting.

Technology and Meetings

We live in a world that seems to be ruled by technology. Further, as technologists, we have a far higher propensity to rely on our gadgets and gizmos to meet the needs of our daily lives than others. I've heard stories of people who have had to travel for business and as one of their carry-on bags brought a monitor. I've heard other stories about someone who came to meetings and brought a laptop, a voice recorder, a monitor, a movie camera, and a tablet computer to make sure that nothing from the meeting was lost. I'm typically known to bring my tablet with me so I can take notes in a meeting. My tablet can't get connectivity at work, so the only purpose I have for bringing it is to make sure I can take notes that will be backed up as soon as I can get online.

Some meetings are conducive to technologies. Some meeting hosts are likewise so inclined. Others, not so much.

On the topic of the use of technology in meetings, remember that it is usually more prudent to keep your cell phone on mute and if possible either in your pocket or with the screen turned to the table. This will remove temptation. This is true not only if you are an invitee to the meeting but also if you are the host. It's particularly disconcerting to attend a meeting held by someone who insists on people not working through the meeting but who then has no problem taking business calls during the meeting or excusing themself to step out into the hallway to take a phone call.

It's not always possible, however, to cut yourself off even for the duration of a meeting. Perhaps your spouse or child is ill, maybe your wife is pregnant and due (or overdue), or you might have a critical project that requires you to be connected at all times. These are special situations. Don't use your phone for surfing or social media. Don't use your laptop for work if you aren't required to check on situations for a project or you aren't on call and need to be connected continuously.

Touch and Personal Space

Personal space and people's reaction to their and others' personal space are as varied as there are people and cultures in the world. Often if you are dealing with another culture, simply getting a heads-up on what to expect is sufficient to prepare yourself for what might be very different from what you are used to.

For example, you might find yourself on a project in Ecuador and your first day on site you meet many of the other people on the same project. Some of the people are from Mexico. Others are from Chile. Still others are from Argentina. It might be helpful for someone to warn you that you are possibly going to be the recipient of cheek kisses from several of the other members of the team. It's not anything untoward, simply a cultural artifact.

Eye contact is something that I've always had problems with. I have had to make a conscious effort to make eye contact when I am talking to people. I've had to work at it to such an extent that I notice when people avoid making eye contact with me. I've also had to make an effort, however, to make sure that I don't offend people when I'm talking to them by making eye contact in the wrong situations or by avoiding eye contact in other situations.

Asian cultures, for example, find it respectful to not engage in eye contact, whereas Latin American and North American cultures place a value on making eye contact as a way to convey additional meaning in a conversation.

In Western European countries you might have to walk a fine line, particularly if you are a woman conversing with a man or a man with a woman. While it is desirable to maintain almost continuous eye contact with the person with whom you are talking in business situations, it can also be considered flirtatious, so you should take care in more casual situations.

In Muslim countries, where religious law dictates that men and women not make and hold eye contact (or in some countries even make eye contact), care should be taken. It can leave people with the wrong impression if a woman holds a man's gaze.

Touch is another personal space and proximity concept that differs between cultures. In the United States, for example, a firm hand shake or a pat on the back is not only accepted but usually an expected way to greet a business colleague. In France or Argentina, it's a cheek kiss (on one or both cheeks). Touching on the head (particularly with children, even children with whom you're not acquainted) is appropriate in North America, but any touch to the head is inappropriate in Asia because the head there is considered to be sacred. In the Middle East, touch or acceptance of a gift or a business card should only ever be done with the right hand as the left hand is relegated to handling bodily hygiene.

Posture, whether standing or seated, is another piece of your countenance to be mindful of in cross-cultural interactions. Western cultures view as acceptable a relaxed seated posture with legs crossed ankle over knee, either leg on top, and their feet pointing either right or left. To sit the same way in the company of people of certain other cultures would cause offense because the bottom of the foot being viewable is considered to be offensive—or dirty like the bottom of the shoe. When meeting with people cross culturally, therefore, it is more acceptable universally to sit with legs either crossed knee over knee or with feet flat on the floor. Many Western men view crossing the legs knee over knee to be somewhat effeminate (because when women cross their legs, this is typically the manner they use) and honestly sometimes to be physically uncomfortable. In Japan and South Korea, crossing legs is not typically acceptable; rather, feet flat, with knees together and level, with straight back and hands on knees is the traditionally acceptable seated posture.

Slouching suggests that you lack confidence at best, but in Taiwan it shows disrespect. Standing with your hands on your hips in Argentina indicates either anger or a challenge, while in the United States it shows an attitude of pride or an attempt at power over the other person in a conversation. When both people in a conversation stand with hands on hips, it is often a sign of preening or a power play.

The use of physical space in different cultures is as different as the cultures themselves. In Japan and China (and other densely populated countries) there is far less need for personal space, and people in these countries are less likely to take offense or react strongly one way or another to accidental jostling or touch. In China, the concept of "lines" or queues is far different than that of the West. It was surprising to me to experience (several years ago) trying to buy a ticket to Temple of the Sun when people in Beijing pushed and elbowed their way to the window with no concept of a row or a queue or anyone waiting their turn. In a country with so many people, you have to do what needs to be done to survive; it is the way that things are done. As a result of there being so many people in limited space, the concept of personal space is as limited as the space. Compare this to people from the United States, where there's the idea that people require their own space. Standing a bit too close to someone means that you are encroaching on their space; in fact, people crouch into the back of the elevator when too many people come in as an attempt to keep their personal space clear. This can make it difficult to have a conversation.

Outside of the Office

When you are not at work but at a social event with your co-workers, it's not the time to be discussing work. Social events are not about business; they are about building relationships and establishing closer connections with others at the event.

There are naturally topics to avoid in such situations. Avoid politics, religion, and anything overly personal. Personal topics can be discussed between close associates but not typically with a large group. It's much safer to talk about the venue for the event, traffic, sports, weather, and even cultural differences if the situation and people are amenable.

If there is a mix of cultures at the event, take your lead from the host or local participants. In general, stay upbeat, or at the very least neutral, and if possible make a point of finding out some of the do's and don'ts of the event and the people attending. Remember, it takes one second to make a memorable mistake, and it can take much longer making amends.

If you are the host or you are a member of the host's team, you should be the one making sure that everyone is kept comfortable and at ease. It is your job to start meetings and any group discussions that may need to arise. Smaller group discussions can take care of themselves, but for the discussion within the group at large, the meeting host should be looked at to lead the discussion.

As the host, you have a larger than normal responsibility to be aware of any social taboos, drinking customs (or taboos), or dietary restrictions that may occur within the group and make arrangements for those difference.

Keep Your Fingers to Yourself

I talk with my hands. I gesture and express myself somewhat larger than life. Sometimes I think that this is a holdover from public speaking classes and contests in high school. I didn't realize how unconscious some of my gestures are until I got caught making one after a meeting as I was walking down the hallway; someone laughed and told me that they knew what that gesture meant and I should be glad that other people in the office didn't. I started to be more cognizant of how other people saw my gesticulations.

Think I'm overreacting? Not really. Consider the simple gesture that, as children, we learned in the United States as meaning OK: the thumb and index finger forming a circle and the remaining three fingers up. How can OK be offensive? If you are from Brazil or Germany, the gesture is considered to be quite offensive because it depicts a body orifice that is not appropriate in polite company. The same gesture in Japan means money, so it possibly might be used in business, but it doesn't have the same connotations that someone from the United States would understand. In France, OK also doesn't mean OK but rather means zero. Think what it might mean if someone from France, Japan, and the United States talk and use the gesture in conversation and what each might be thinking. U.S. President Richard Nixon learned this lesson when he flashed the OK sign (Figure 6-1) in South America and learned that he in effect flipped them what amounted to the offensive single middle finger in the United States.

Figure 6-1. *Hand gesture for "OK"*

What you might consider to be the peace sign or maybe "V" for victory (Figures 6-2 and 6-3) is far from being victorious or peaceful. The sign was coined by Winston Churchill in England circa World War II. What was victorious in the 1940s in England or peaceful in the 1960s in the United States (depending on whether it is flashed with palm facing away from you or facing toward yourself) can signify far less benevolent meanings. If you show the sign palm out, it means victory or peace, but with the palm facing in in Australia, the UK, and other countries across the globe, it is a rude gesture that is not appropriate in polite company.

Figure 6-2. *Sign for peace or victory, palm in*

Figure 6-3. *Sign for peace or victory, palm out*

I have lived in Austin, Texas, and I completely understood what U.S. President George W. Bush meant in 2005 on his Inauguration Day when he gestured with his index and pinky finger extended from his fist to show the world the infamous "hook 'em horns" gesture (Figures 6-4 and 6-5). This gesture in Austin is the Texas Longhorn football symbol. He was simply doing what came naturally as an ex-governor of Texas. What he didn't realize was that the global community didn't have the same understanding of the symbolism that he did. The same gesture, if you are in a concert venue, implies "ROCK ON, dudes," but internationally it does not rock. In fact, in Italy it signifies that a man's wife is cheating on him, and in Africa and several other countries it is as offensive as the OK symbol is in others. In still other countries (Mediterranean countries, for example), it is a satanic symbol.

Figure 6-4. *Sign for Longhorn football*

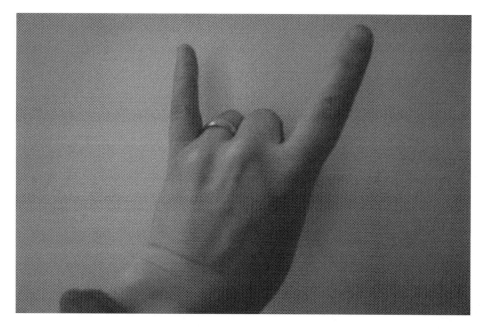

Figure 6-5. *Sign for Longhorn football*

Thumbs-up is safe, right (Figure 6-6)? All it means is "good job," right? Or sometimes it means asking for a ride if you're along the road hitchhiking. Not exactly. While it does mean these things in many countries and cultures, it also is an insult in Australia, Greece, and many Middle Eastern cultures. There it signifies that you are telling your audience the equivalent of the offensive "up yours" gesture in the United States. And if you think that is the only drawback (as if that isn't bad enough) to the sign, consider it as a number to anyone counting on their fingers. In Germany it is the number 1, in Japan it is the number 5, and in ASL (another culture that you really need to take into account when using your hands to express yourself) it is the number 10. There can be significant issues when people look at your symbols and completely misunderstand your meaning.

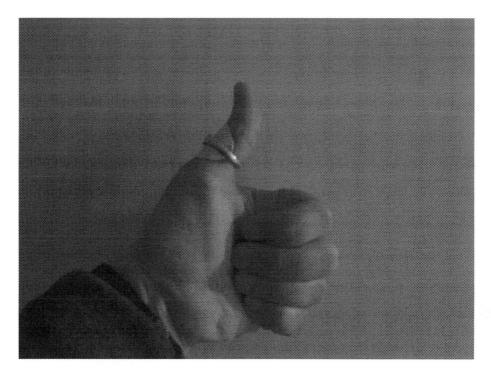

Figure 6-6. *Sign for thumbs-up*

Need to gesture to point something out to someone or to a group? Pointing with the index finger is something that is relatively common (Figure 6-7) . You point to a passage on a printed page. You point out the directions you would like others to follow. You point out details while you are giving a presentation. Using your index finger to point in Asia and Latin America (among other places) is offensive and rude. It's impolite in even more countries. When I was a child, we learned in school that when you point with your index finger at someone or something, you need to remember that there are three fingers pointing back at you, and you should make sure that you are not pointing out something of which you should take heed. When gesturing in the situations where you would ordinarily point with your index finger, it would be better to take the tactic that is taught to the cast members at Disneyland: "point" with your open hand or with two fingers (index and middle finger) (Figure 6-8) so as to not offend. It takes a little practice to cull this gesture from your habits, but it will garner much more favor with anyone in any culture than the alternative.

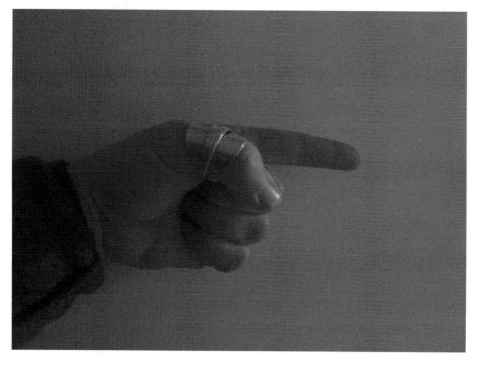

Figure 6-7. *Sign for pointing*

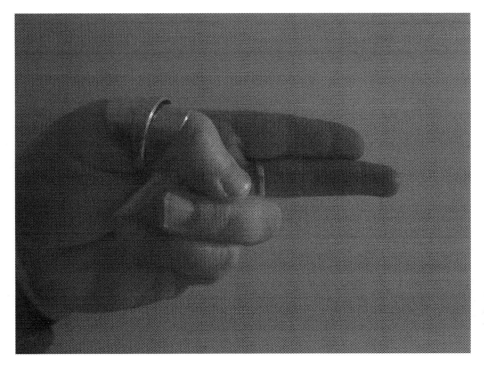

Figure 6-8. *Sign for pointing at Disneyland*

Need to try to get someone to come closer? Typically, people in the United States would curl their index finger with their palm facing up (Figure 6-9). This is common enough, particularly when you're trying to get your child to come closer when they are in trouble. That's the time I most remember seeing it used in my direction. Again, in Asian countries and many other parts of the world, it is extremely rude. In many Asian countries it is used only when beckoning dogs (so using it with people implies that you are relegating them to the status of dog), and in the Philippines it is a gesture that could get you a broken finger or land you in jail. In Singapore, it is used to signify death. The appropriate way to beckon someone in many countries is to face your palm toward the ground, curl your fingers under, and move your fingers in a scratching motion (Figure 6-10).

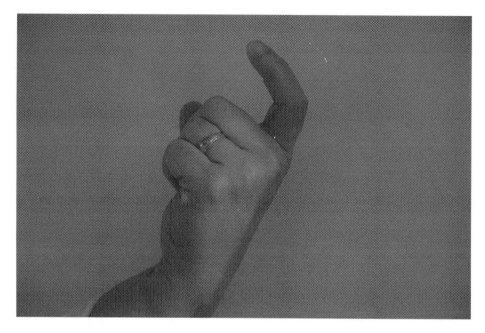

Figure 6-9. *Sign to come closer, considered rude in some places*

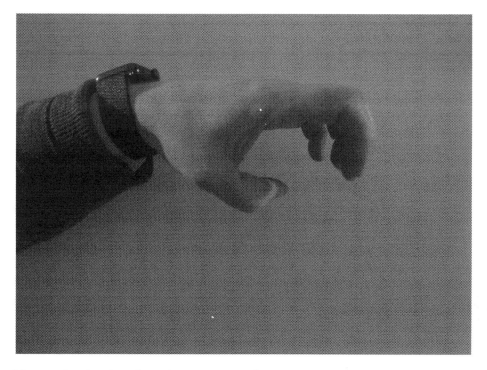

Figure 6-10. *Another sign to come closer*

Curb your desire to wave open-handed with fingers slightly opened (Figure 6-11). This gesture can be misinterpreted not as hello but as an insult or that you are saying enough, stop right there, or as my kids would have said when they were in school "Talk to the hand because the face ain't listening." Worse, in Greece the gesture is used to imply that the person using it wishes the recipient to "eat feces."

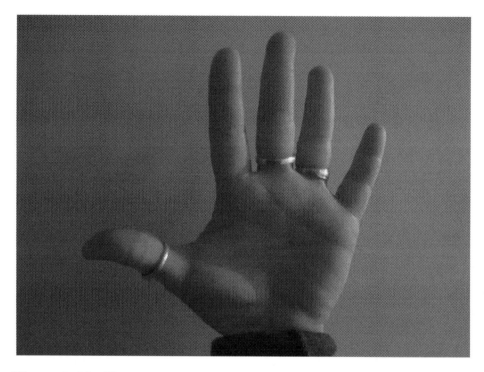

Figure 6-11. *Sign to wave*

Curb the desire to look at your watch. Even if you're wearing a watch that is tied to your phone and you are checking to see what e-mail or text message just came in, resist the urge. It will wait. Looking at your watch implies that you're in a hurry, that you have better things to do, or that you have better places to be. It is rude under good circumstances, and cross culturally you need to remember that communication is important, it can take time, and it is never good to leave people thinking that they are not important enough for you to give your whole attention.

Crossing your fingers to entice good luck or good fortune? Not so fast. While the crossed fingers gesture originated in Pagan religions as a means to ward off evil, it also has been used behind your back to indicate that you want not to experience bad ramifications from "a little white lie." In general, it is best not to be seen crossing your fingers. Also, there are places in the world where the crossed finger gesture implies a part of the female anatomy that is not socially appropriate.

Key Takeaways and Lessons Learned

It's important to remember that when talking face to face much more information is conveyed to the audience. This can be beneficial in helping with understanding. It can also be detrimental because it can lead to misunderstandings. I know myself that I have a very expressive face, which isn't always a good thing.

Be careful with hand gestures; you never know when they will be misunderstood.

Remember, a smile translates well, even over the phone. Even if you don't mean it, smile when you're talking on the phone, and it's OK to take a deep breath and prepare yourself for the discussion when you are talking.

References for Further Reading

"The Guide to Hand Gestures Around the World." Huffington Post. https://www.huffingtonpost.com/2014/03/17/the-global-guide-to-hand-_n_4956860.html.

"Gestures to Avoid in Cross-Cultural Business: In Other Words, Keep Your Fingers to Yourself!" Huffington Post. https://www.huffingtonpost.com/gayle-cotton/cross-cultural-gestures_b_3437653.html.

Lee, Stephanie. "8 Common American Gestures That'll Confuse the Sh*t Out of People Overseas." Thrillist, 2017. https://www.thrillist.com/travel/nation/reading-body-language-hand-signals-gestures-meanings-other-countries.

"What Hand Gestures Mean in Different Countries." Busuu Blog. `https://blog.busuu.com/what-hand-gestures-mean-in-different-countries/`.

"Rude hand gestures of the world (don't try these on holiday)." The Telegraph. 2017, `www.telegraph.co.uk/travel/galleries/Rude-hand-gestures-of-the-world/`.

"8 Telephone Etiquette Tips." Advanced Etiquette Training and Consulting in International Business Protocol and Social Etiquette. `www.advancedetiquette.com/2012/01/8-telephone-etiquette-tips/`.

"Telephone Etiquette." OfficeSkills.org Blog. `http://officeskills.org/telephone_etiquette.html`

"The 5 Most Important Rules of Proper Telephone Etiquette." Humanity Blog. `https://www.humanity.com/blog/the-5-most-important-rules-of-proper-telephone-etiquette.html`.

Index

A

American Sign Language
(ASL), 37, 39–40

B

British Sign Language (BSL), 39–40

C

Caller ID, 108
Casual contact, 32
Cleveland Institute of Art, 104
Colloquialisms, 89, 95
Communication
    Brazil, 13
    business, 2
    business people, 12
    colloquialism, 89
    company, 11
    conversation, 3
    culture (*see* Culture)
    different situations, 1
    emojis, 96
    England, 13
    exchange information, 3

face-to-face communication
    (*see* Face-to-face
    communication)
host country, 14
human-to-human, 107
humor (*see* Humor)
idioms (*see* Idioms)
interaction, 9
Jargon and acronyms, 101–104
judgmental of things, 11
listening and attention, 15
local language, 10
media, 14
national/international
    borders, 15
native language, 9
non-native speakers, 9
nonverbal, 3
phone (*see* Telephone
    communication)
professional career, 3
rough language, 98, 100–101
self-confidence, 1
shortcuts, 96
slang (*see* Slang)
South Africa, 11

135

© April Wells 2018
A. Wells, *The Tech Professional's Guide to Communicating in a Global Workplace*,
https://doi.org/10.1007/978-1-4842-3471-6

Get the eBook for only $5!

Why limit yourself?

With most of our titles available in both PDF and ePUB format, you can access your content wherever and however you wish—on your PC, phone, tablet, or reader.

Since you've purchased this print book, we are happy to offer you the eBook for just $5.

To learn more, go to http://www.apress.com/companion or contact support@apress.com.

 *For the Complete Technology & Database Professional*

IOUG represents the **voice of Oracle technology and database professionals** - empowering you to be **more productive in your business** and career by delivering education, sharing **best practices** and providing technology direction and networking opportunities.

Context, Not Just Content

IOUG is dedicated to helping our members become an #IOUGenius by staying on the cutting-edge of Oracle technologies and industry issues through practical content, user-focused education, and invaluable networking and leadership opportunities:

- *SELECT Journal* is our quarterly publication that provides in-depth, peer-reviewed articles on industry news and best practices in Oracle technology

- Our #IOUGenius blog highlights a featured weekly topic and provides content driven by Oracle professionals and the IOUG community

- Special Interest Groups provide you the chance to collaborate with peers on the specific issues that matter to you and even take on leadership roles outside of your organization

- COLLABORATE is our once-a-year opportunity to connect with the members of not one, but three, Oracle users groups (IOUG, OAUG and Quest) as well as with the top names and faces in the Oracle community.

Who we are...

... **more than 20,000** database professionals, developers, application and infrastructure architects, business intelligence specialists and IT managers

... **a community of users** that share experiences and knowledge on issues and technologies that matter to you and your organization

Interested? Join IOUG's community of Oracle technology and database professionals at www.ioug.org/Join.

Independent Oracle Users Group | phone: (312) 245-1579 | email: membership@ioug.org
330 N. Wabash Ave., Suite 2000, Chicago, IL 60611

Printed in the United States
By Bookmasters